*T*he Palauan Gods decided that who could throw his betelnut the furthest would own the island Ngerduais in Airai. The God Medechii Belau cheated by putting a Chesisebangiau bird in his hand, which is the same color as chewed betelnut. When he threw it, the little red bird spread its wings and flew all the way to the island, winning the contest and the island for the God.

Tommy E. Remengesau, Jr.
President

Republic of Palau
Office of the President

Dear Reader,

Within these pages you will find photographs and information on the birds and bats that inhabit our island nation of Palau. This book is the first of its kind in Palau and I commend Ms. Etpison and Mr. Pratt on this important undertaking.

Palau is mostly known throughout the world for the beauty and diversity of its marine environment. But there are other natural wonders that make Palau so unique. This comprehensive work highlights some of Palau's most beautiful, yet least known natural treasures.

This book is a reminder of Palau's seemingly boundless capacity to amaze us. Even those of us who have spent our lives in the jungles and on the waters here will learn something of Palau's birds and flying mammals from this book. This knowledge will bring a newfound appreciation for the animals that inhabit the skies above, and with it a commitment to their preservation.

I trust you will enjoy this book as much as I do. And on behalf of all Palauans, I invite you to visit Palau and discover for yourself the many natural wonders of our island home.

Sincerely,

Tommy E. Remengesau, Jr.
President of the Republic of Palau

r many years the Palau Conservation Society has worked
h local communities to protect Palau's unique natural
itage. The illustrated *Field Guide to the Birds of Palau* has
en our main reference book on Palau birds, but since it was
tten 20 years ago, much has changed in Palau, both in our
vironment and our increased knowledge of Palau's birds.
erefore, we were very excited to hear about the publication
this first photographic guidebook, and it is with great
asure that we can hereby introduce "Birds and Bats of
lau", which does not only showcase the different species
nd here, but includes many never before published photo-
aphs of the behavior and nesting of our resident and endemic
d and bat species.

some of Palau's largest terrestrial fauna, birds provide
portant ecosystem services by dispersing seeds and pollen,
d regulating insects and smaller animal populations through
edation. Bird deposits over time on the islands of Peleliu and
gaur enabled phosphate mining there in the early part of this
ntury, and bird watching is a small but rapidly growing part of
lau's tourism industry today.

of Palau's endemic birds use forests during some or all of
eir lives. The current rate of forest loss is unknown. Proposed
velopment projects throughout Palau may lead to increased
est loss through fragmentation, introduction of invasive
ecies, and increased fires. Swamp forests in Palau are the
st diverse in Micronesia, but are limited in extent and distri-
tion. Marshes and cultivated wetland taro patches are also
dely distributed but generally small in size. These rare fresh-
ter wetland habitats are important for a variety of bird
ecies.

2004, PCS had the privilege to work with partners from
ound Palau and the Pacific region to conduct a national
rvey of Palau's birds. This survey helped us to identify areas
at qualify as potential Globally Important Bird Areas because
their ability to provide critical habitat for endemic, endan-
red, or nesting birds.

e would like to thank BirdLife International, the US Fish and
ldlife Service, and the Global Environment Facility Small
ants Program, who collectively made it possible for PCS to
ntribute to the publication of this much needed book. This will
a reference guide for both local and tourist birders for years
come.

Palau Conservation Society
P.O.Box 1811, Koror Palau PW96940
Email: pcs@palaunet.com
www.palau-pcs.org

Palau Conservation
Society

BirdLife
INTERNATIONAL

GEF

U.S.
FISH & WILDLIFE
SERVICE

www.palau.panpacific.com

Shell Palau

ISBN-10: 1-56647-871-5
ISBN-13: 978-1-56647-871-7
Library of Congress Control Number: 2008925658

PHOTO CREDITS
Photographs in this book are by Mandy T. Etpison, unless oth・
indicated on individual photos. Contributing photographe・

Thomas Dove
H. Douglas Pratt
Michelle & Peter Wong
Eric VanderWerf
Patrick L. Colin
Martin Hale
Daphne Gemmill
Shallum Etpison
Bert Yates
Paul Pisano
Jacob Faust
Dan Vice
Deane P. Lewis, http://dl.id.au
Selina Caroll
Marjorie Falanruw
Ian Montgomery/ Birdway Pty, Ltd.
Helen Reef Conservation Program

Aerial maps by Palaris,
courtesy Palau Ministry of Resources & Development
Palauan artifacts, old prints and Charlie Gibbons painting
courtesy Etpison Museum

Etpison
Museum

Mutual Publishing, L.L.C
1215 Center Street, Suite 210
Honolulu, HI 96816
Ph: 808-732-1709 / Fax: 808-734-4094
email: info@mutualpublishing.com
www.mutualpublishing.com

Printed in Korea

the
Birds & Bats
of
Palau

by

H. Douglas Pratt
and
Mandy T. Etpison

with an Appendix by
Eric VanderWerf

Bird Paintings by
H. Douglas Pratt

Photography and Design by
Mandy T. Etpison

CONTENTS

BIRDS OF FORESTS, OPEN COUNTRY AND VILLAGES

BIRDS OF PONDS AND WETLANDS

SHOREBIRDS

ACKNOWLEDGEMENTS

We are grateful to:

Palau Pacific Resort
Palau Conservation Society
Shell Palau
Etpison Museum
Neco Marine Dive/ Tour
Palau Postal Service
Palau Government
for their financial contributions,
encouragement, and support:

A special thanks to:

the photographers
who permitted use of their
work without charge;

to

Dr. Eric VanderWerf
who provided both a report of his
surveys with PCS and photos;

and to the

**North Carolina State Museum
of Natural Sciences**,
and the Friends of the Museum,
for support of HDP's research
and writing.

AUTHORS' PREFACE

I first visited Palau in 1976 on the first of two expeditions gather information for a new field guide to birds of the tropic Pacific, and fell in love with the place. On that trip, my colleagu Delwyn Berrett and Phillip L.Bruner of Brigham Young Unive sity- Hawaii Campus and I met Bob Owen, Chief Conservation for the trust Territory of the Pacific islands, who had been obser ing birds in Palau for several years and who was the first perso to do any meaningful ornithological work on Micronesia sinc World War II. Bruner and I returned in 1978, and worked wi John Engbring who had joined Owen as a U.S. Peace Corps o nithologist. These research efforts resulted in a number of scie tific papers, as well as first-ever recordings of all of Palau's e demic bird voices, which are now archived in the Macaula Libray of the Cornell Lab of Ornithology in Ithaca, New Yor USA. Ultimately all of this work was summarized in *A Field Guic to the Birds of Hawaii and the Tropical Pacific* (Pratt et al. 1987 which is now undergoing revision. I have now visited Palau dozen times in various capacities, and I continue to be fasc nated by its unique and unusual birdlife, not to mention its spe tacular scenery. It remains my favorite place in Micronesia n only because of its varied indigenous avifauna, but because its great potential as a "migrant trap" where anything can turn u I first became aware of Mandy Etpison's amazing photographs 2004, through a mutual friend, Tom Dove M.D., who was at th time with the US Army in Honolulu. After several years of corr spondence, I finally met Mandy in 2007, and agreed to write text for her bird and bat book. I am deeply honored that sh chose me for this task, because she is truly a world-class pho tographer. Her photos document the natural history of Palau birds in a way that mere words could not. She clearly loves h subject, and her careful observations have been incorporate throughout the text of this book, so it is truly a co-authorship. have tried to cover a lot of bases in my writing, hoping to mak the book accessible to beginners and high school students a well as informative to more sophisticated readers. Where po sible, I explain technical terminology to help students learn n only how to identify Palau's birds, but also a little basic ornithc ogy. I have also kept in mind the birding tourists who are visitin Palau in increasing numbers these days. Much of the informatio presented herein, especially the photo-documentation of bree ing biology, is new, and because this book is not a peer-reviewe scientific publication, Mandy and I are preparing a techni paper to be submitted to an appropriate journal. We anticipa that this book will be a vehicle for illustrations to supplement th report. A picture is, after all, worth a thousand words.

H. Douglas Pratt, Ph.[
Research Curator of Bird
North Carolina State Museum of Natural Science
doug.pratt@ncmail.n

...e Doug, I fell in love with Palau when I first visited in 1984. ...hen I returned to work here in 1985, I also fell in love with my ...ture husband, which explains why I am still here today... I didn't ...ally get interested in birds until I was preparing my third book ...Palau in 2004, in which I wanted to show more than just the ...arine life Palau is famous for. I had admired Doug's bird illus-...tions for years, and when I started asking around for an expert ...Palauan birds, his name kept coming up, so I started emailing ...m for information on current bird names. When I published my ...rdcover bookset *Palau, Natural & Cultural History* in 2004, a ...: of local people expressed interest in the bird photos, and ...ked about the need for a smaller softcover photo ID book that ...ur operators would be able to use to inform tourists and train ...cal tour guides and students about Palauan birds. I was very ...ppy Doug agreed to work on the book with me, since I really ...dn't know enough about birds to single-handedly do a whole ...ook on them. Rather than just do a simple ID guidebook with a ...zzy picture of each bird and two lines of text, I really wanted to ...y and show more in-depth information on the biology of the ...rds, and show photographs, especially of the unique endemic ...d Micronesian species, that really portray the character and ...ehavior of each bird. Of course, I didn't really appreciate at the ...ne how poorly known a lot of these species are, even by Palau-...is and scientists, and that there are few professional photos ...railable for most Micronesian species. I had to become a better ...rd photographer in a hurry, and getting the over 670 photo-...aphs you see in this book kept me busy for two years and ...ught me a lot about photography and birds. My favorite sub-...cts, which clearly shows in this book, are the resident forest ...d true seabirds. I am very grateful to Doug for patiently teach-...g me about the waders, winter visitors to Palau that all look ...ke to me, and which I find totally frustrating to identify and pho-...graph. I sent him endless email attachments of waders and mi-...ants to ID, which I'm sure would have exasperated most orni-...ologists, but Doug patiently emailed me back every time. He ...lded that getting bird photos by email from me was like opening ...esents on Christmas morning, which motivated me to go back ...it and get more photographs... I certainly enjoyed working on ...is project, and hope it will assist Palau in creating more bird ...d conservation awareness, and development of birdwatching ...urism. Eventhough I'm going to take a break from birds now ...d return to underwater photography, I'll be sure to keep an eye ...it for nests and rare winter migrants for our next edition of this ...ook, and so should you birders out there, since new and un-...sual things are reported from Palau on a regular basis!

...andy Thijssen Etpison
...anaging Director
...tpison Museum & Gallery
...pison@palaunet.com   www.necomarine.com

ACKNOWLEDGEMENTS

Doug
I would like to acknowledge the early influence and support of the late Robert P.Owen, and the field assistance and com-panionship of John Engbring and John Kochi. A number of other individuals have been helpful in one way or another to my work in Palau, including Phillip L. Bruner, Delwyn Ber-rett, Gary Wiles, the late Robert L. Pyle, Paul Pisano, Daphne Gemmill, Marjorie Fa-lanruw, and Lazarena Yoshi-nao. Louisiana State Univer-sity Museum of Natural Sci-ence for many years provided my institutional base.

Mandy
I would like to thank my always supportive husband Shallum, for putting up with this latest project of mine. Also my son Iked and his cousins, for allow-ing me to combine their Rock Island trips with my birding. A special thanks to all the Palau-ans who showed me nest loca-tions, to Benito for bringing me the Nightjar, and to Tilus for finding me the elusive White-browed Crake. It was a sur-prise to find out Tom Dove became a great bird photogra-pher in the years we had not seen each other, and the monopod he gave me helped take a lot of the photographs you see here, thanks, Tom!

INTRODUCTION

The Republic of Palau (aka Belau in the Palauan language) comprises about 586 islands, with a total land area of 456 sq.km that form the western extremity of Micronesia. Only 11 of the islands are inhabited. Lying closer to such larger islands as the Philippines and New Guinea, Palau is biologically richer and more diverse than the rest of Micronesia, with a large number of species found nowhere else (= endemics). It is also strategically positioned near major migratory paths for birds, and boasts a long list of seasonal visitors and rare vagrants that spice up the offerings for birders. Considered one of the world's great scenic and natural wonders, and famous among scuba divers, Palau is becoming slowly known to general travelers around the globe, especially since it became the site for 2 cycles of the popular American TV show Survivor. Palau had 88,175 visitors in 2007.

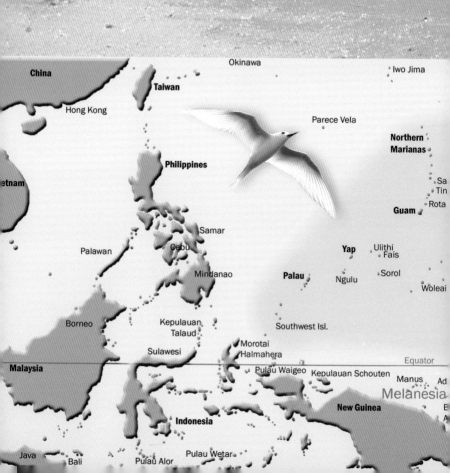

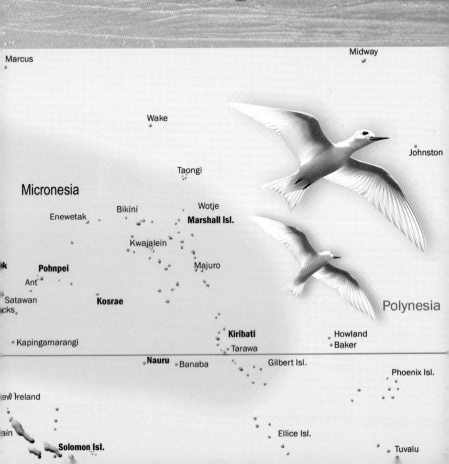

After Palau first became known to the outside world in the 1500s, it was only sporadically visited by trading ships. It has endured a long history of colonial rule by Spanish, Germans, Japanese and Americans, since outside contact increased in the 19th century. The indigenous population was reduced to a tenth of its former size by alien diseases, and was reduced further during World War II, when Palau was occupied by the Japanese, then bombed and partially invaded by the Americans in 1944. After the war, the United States assumed control under a UN Trusteeship, and the Japanese were repatriated. Palau voted to separate politically from the rest of Micronesia in 1978, but did not become fully independent until 1994, after signing a Compact of Free Association with the US. The current population is around 19,129, of which 13,209 are native Palauans.

Marcus

Midway

Wake

Johnston

Taongi

Micronesia

Enewetak

Bikini

Wotje

Marshall Isl.

Kwajalein

Pohnpei

Majuro

Ant

Satawan
cks

Kosrae

Polynesia

Kapingamarangi

Kiribati

Howland

Tarawa

Baker

Nauru

Banaba

Gilbert Isl.

Phoenix Isl.

ew Ireland

ain

Solomon Isl.

Ellice Isl.

Tuvalu

The Palau archipelago includes three different kinds of islands: ancient volcanic, limestone (coral), and atolls. The main islands, mostly enclosed with a single reef system, include the larger volcanic islands to the north, and the famous "Rock Islands" to the south. The volcanic islands have highly eroded soils and low, hilly terrain (maximum elevation ca. 700 ft or 213 m).

Palau has no mountains. The Rock Islands are actually ancient coral reefs that have been uplifted by geological forces. The islands of Peleliu, at the south end of the main reef, and Angaur, which lies just outside it, are relatively flat raised limestone platforms. Scattered 300 km to the southwest are four other tiny raised coral islands, and one true atoll. Two other atolls lie north of the main islands. Some islands, like Koror and Babeldaob, incorporate both volcanic and limestone formations.

Lying just north of the equator, Palau enjoys a tropical climate with average temperature of 74-83 F and relative humidity averaging 82%. Annual rainfall is around 150 in, and though the islands lie outside the main typhoon tracks which are to the north, they get their share of severe storms when typhoons pass by Yap or Guam.

The larger Palauan islands are mostly forested, the kind of forest depending on the substrate. Mangrove forests and Nypa palm swamps occupy shallow areas along the shoreline. Some of the mangrove areas are quite extensive and are the most species-rich in Micronesia for both plants and animals. Inland, true rainforest can be found, especially along streams and in ravines. On exposed hilltops, the forest may open up into savannahs characterized by ferns, grasses, and scattered Pandanus trees. Some savannahs are natural, while others are the result of extensive logging of the forest during Japanese times, followed by erosion and frequent fires that prevented forest regrowth. Around towns and villages, the natural vegetation has largely been supplanted by agroforest, a vegetation type that, though natural-looking, is made up mostly of introduced trees useful to people such as coconut, breadfruit, papaya, betel nut palm, banana and mango.

Forests on the limestone islands and atolls have distinctive species components compared to forests on volcanic soils. Because the Rock Islands are so rugged, with very little soil, their forests have never been logged or cut down for agriculture, and they remain nearly pristine today. The only obvious manmade changes are the introduction of mammalian predators such as rats, and palm-destroying cockatoos. These unspoiled limestone forests are one of Palau's greatest natural treasures.

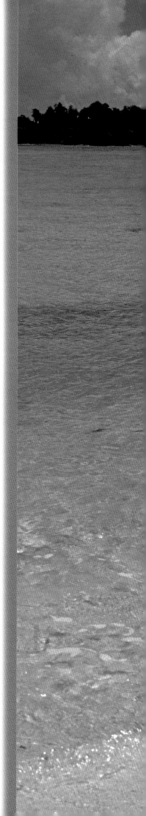

N   Palau

Velasco reef

Ngeruangel

Kayangel

Kossol

Babeldaob

West passage

Koror

Lighthouse channel

Rock Islands

German
channel

Peleliu

Angaur   Southwest Islands 300+ km

Palau's Avifauna

Palau has by far the richest native bird community
Micronesia. Breeding land and freshwater birds include re
sentatives of 19 families, while seabirds add another 6. Th
residents are joined every year by migrants that come to P
after nesting elsewhere. Some come from the north during
northern winter months, while a smaller number come
Australia during the northern summer. Particularly impor
among these regular visitors are ducks, herons and egrets,
shorebirds, but Palau also receives many land bird visitors
cluding raptors and songbirds. Almost every year, somet
new is added to the Palau list.

Most Palau land birds are endemic at some level (specie
subspecies), but all are descended from colonizers from e
where. When a bird reaches an isolated island or archipel
such as Palau, it must adapt to the unique conditions it f
here. The population is cut off from its former gene pool, ar
no longer influenced by it or contributing to it. Inevitably
time, the island birds develop distinctive differences. Eventu
they become so different that they would no longer be able t
terbreed with their ancestral population, which has itself b
evolving independently in the meantime, and at that point
have become an endemic species. The process is slow,
birds pass through a "gray zone" in which they may differ
related birds elsewhere, but not enough to keep them from
entering their ancestral gene pool if they had the chance. Th
are endemic subspecies. Just where to draw the line is so
times hard to determine, and may be controversial. The pa
ings by HDP on page 27 depict Palau's endemic species
potential species.

Ngeruangel and Kayangel Atolls

Palau has 3 atolls, Ngeruangel and Kayangel in the north,
Helen Reef in the remote Southwest Islands. The small c
rubble islet of Ngeruangel is a submerged reef, uninhab
and home to a small breeding colony of Swift Terns. The
rounding Velasco reef is a popular fishing area for locals. A
5.5 miles to the southeast are the four islands of Kayangel A
The largest and only inhabited island, Kayangel, has about
residents, while the second-largest uninhabited island, N
ungs, is an important nesting area for the Palau Megap
Young frigatebirds and boobies can be seen fishing arc
these islands, but only nest in the Southwest Islands and
Kayangel can only be reached with the state ferry boat, c
chartering a boat or helicopter. There are no hotels, and per
sion is needed to camp or stay with local families. You will
to bring your own gear/ supplies. Call the Kayangel State o
first to check on current permits, fees and lodging possibi
before planning a visit to these islands.

Patrick L.Colir

Selina Carrol

Patrick L.Colin

Patrick L.Colin

Babeldaob

Palau's "Big Island" is the second largest (332 km2) in Micronesia after Guam. It is mostly rolling hills of deep red v__ canic soil, but at the southern tip includes some bits of uplift__ coral limestone similar in structure to the Rock Islands. Babe__ aob has Palau's only permanent rivers and streams, as well __ numerous coastal bays and estuaries. Waterfalls can be fou__ in the states of Airai, Ngchesar, Ngatpang, Ngeremlengui, a__ Ngardmau. The island is divided into ten states, thinly pop__ lated and with a rural character, although that may change __ services for the new national capital at Melekeok are dev__ oped, and with the finished Compact Road, that now circ__ the island. Extensive areas of relatively undisturbed rainfore__ remain, and the island has most of Palau's savannahs. T__ open grassy lawns around the Capitol and the Palau Airp__ are good places to look for rare migratory birds. Towards Ai__ village, the extensive taro patches along the road are home __ Buff-banded Rails and Purple Swamphens, as well as mig__ tory shorebirds such as Swinhoe's Snipe. Other good birdi__ localities include the following:

Lake Ngardok (left) is the largest natural lake in Micrones__ and the best place to see Common Moorhens in Palau. It __ a natural reserve with a beautiful forest trail to the lakesho__ The trail is indicated by a sign on the left side of the road__ little past the entrance to the Capitol in Melekeok.

The **Jungle River Boat Cruise** is a newly opened boat to__ in Ngchesar State where you can see birds, fruit bats, a__ saltwater crocodiles along the river.

The **Ngatpang Aquaculture Ponds** and nearby lagoon sh__ lows are one of the best places in Palau to look for migrato__ shorebirds, waterfowl and egrets. They can be reached __ turning left onto a dirt road after passing the Daewoo constru__ tion camp on the western leg of the Compact road, which en__ at the Ngatpang village dock.

The **Koror Reservoir** in Airai State attracts migratory wate__ fowl and shorebirds, and the surrounding forest is rich in bird__ To reach it, drive past the airport entrance and follow the d__ road to the left past a construction camp. Before the next tu__ to the right is a locked gate on your left where you can pa__ and walk down to the reservoir.

The top of **Ngerchelchuus** in Ngardmau State is the highe__ peak in Palau at 713 ft. Following the rough dirt road to the t__ you can hang out to enjoy the view, and have a good chan__ to spot the Palau Woodswallows that are permanent resider__ there.

Check with the state offices on current fees and permits.

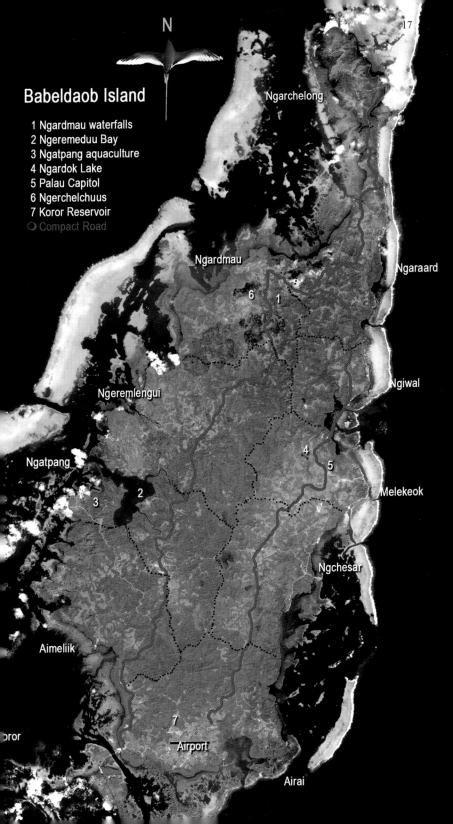

Babeldaob Island

1 Ngardmau waterfalls
2 Ngeremeduu Bay
3 Ngatpang aquaculture
4 Ngardok Lake
5 Palau Capitol
6 Ngerchelchuus
7 Koror Reservoir
○ Compact Road

N

Ngarchelong

Ngaraard

Ngardmau

6   1

Ngiwal

Ngeremlengui

4

5

Ngatpang

Melekeok

2

3

Ngchesar

Aimeliik

7

oror

Airport

Airai

The Koror Complex

South of Babeldaob, and connected by bridge lies the islar Koror and its satellites Arakebesang and Malakal, inter nected by causeways. This area forms the population and c mercial center of Palau, and includes both volcanic and stone portions. Each island still has at least some uninha forest, usually on limestone substrates. Consequently, ma Palau's endemic forest birds can be seen right around t Limestone caves harbor Palau Swiftlets and Palau Sheath-t bats. Palau Owls can be heard calling at night all over K from limestone forests. Koror and eastern Arakebesang are main residential areas, while Malakal boasts the comme port and most of the tour operators and boat docks. Hotels, taurants and stores are found throughout the complex.

Despite urbanization, the Koror complex has several exce birding sites. At low tide, the **flats between Koror and Bal daob** are good for plovers, sandpipers, curlews and god herons and egrets. The flats can be viewed from several pull on both sides of the channel. A spotting scope is essential.

Surprisingly, the best bird spot in downtown Koror is the K landfill adjacent to the aquarium and the Landmark Ma Hotel. A road circles the dump on 3 sides, for easy view access. Rufous Night Herons and Cattle Egrets are very proachable here, and from November to April flocks of Ye Wagtails are usually present. The coral spoil banks east o dump are favorite resting places for tattlers, plovers, and la sandpipers. The landfill and vicinity have produced a long li vagrants over the years.

The best birding on **Malakal** is at the **sewage treatment po** at the very end of the road to the right. The facility is modern odor-free, unlike the landfill, and open during daylight hours. two settling ponds provide habitat for shorebirds, herons, eg and even some rare songbirds. Recent rarities have incl Green Sandpiper, Richard's Pipit, Gray Wagtail, and Orie Reed Warbler.

On **Arakebesang**, the luxurious **Palau Pacific Resort** h beautiful **nature trail** that winds through varied habitats inc ing some good rainforest. Bamboo thickets on the hotel grou harbor seldom-seen Slaty-legged Crakes, and the beachfro a good place to look for lagoon birds. Migratory songbirds be found in the *Casuarina* trees. One does not have to be r tered guest to visit, but be sure to check in at the front desk i want to explore the grounds and nature trail.

A walking tour of the **Dolphins Pacific facility** (5 minute boat from Malakal) can also be combined with birding. It i cated in a Rock Island lagoon, and a lot of the endemic bird cies can be seen around their Emerald lagoon area. Call ticket office on Koror for available tour times/ prices.

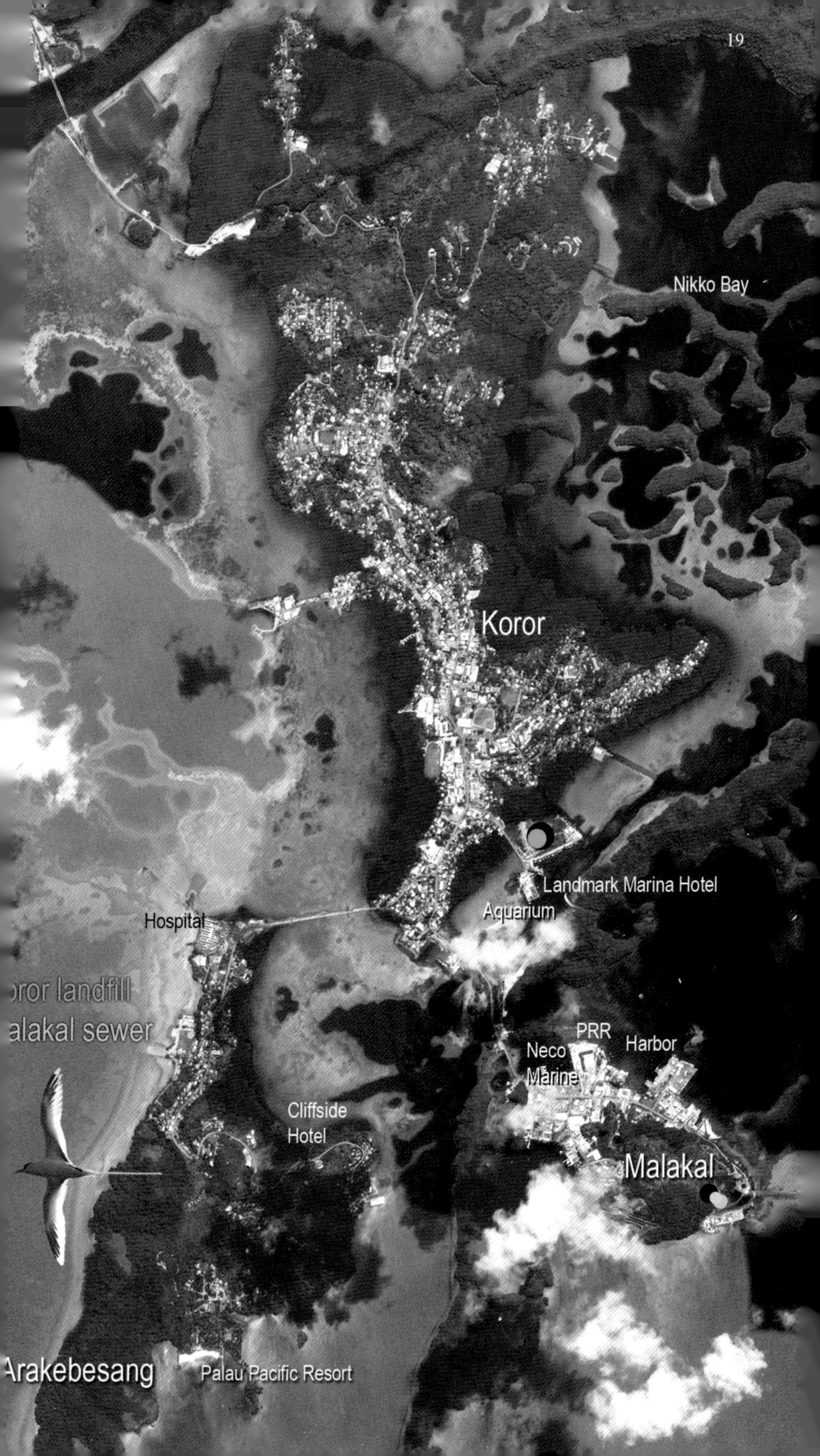

Nikko Bay

Koror

Landmark Marina Hotel

Aquarium

Hospital

oror landfill
alakal sewer

PRR
Neco   Harbor
Marine

Cliffside
Hotel

Malakal

Arakebesang   Palau Pacific Resort

The Rock Islands

Palau is famous for its spectacular Rock Islands and their s
rounding shallow lagoons. Unique in all the world, they rem
a stunningly beautiful place to go snorkeling, diving, kayaki
birding, or fishing. The visitors they attract are an import
part of Palau's economy. When the crystal clear lagoon wat
flow over white sand, they produce vivid turquoise reflectic
that color the underparts of tropicbirds and terns so that th
look blue instead of white, and give the entire area the look
some ethereal fairyland.

The islands are an ancient coral reef that has been uplift
above the sea, and thus are literally made of limestone ro
with virtually no soil. At the waterline, the rock is slowly be
undercut by the action of chitons and other organisms. As
result, many of the smaller islets resemble mushrooms, a
landing is difficult. Fortunately, numerous small sandy bea
es are scattered around where one can land a boat and
ashore. Because there is little soil, no fresh water, and no
terrain suitable for agriculture, these islands have remair
largely free of human settlement and other disturbance. E
spite the lack of soil, the rugged terrain is covered by der
forest, its roots clinging to the jagged rock surface. The limit
soil that accumulates in crevices is mostly decaying orga
matter, and direct rainfall is sufficient to promote lush growt

The forest has a characteristic mix of native trees includi
the endemic palm *Gulubia palauensis*, which sadly has be
virtually eliminated by introduced parrots and cockatoos th
eat the terminal bud, killing the whole tree. Otherwise, the f
est is essentially as it has always been, and forms a natu
sanctuary for Palau's terrestrial wildlife. One area, **Ngeruku**
Islands Wildlife Preserve, also has rigid legal protection,
not open to tourists or locals, and visits are by special per
only.

Among birds, the endemic Giant White-eye is notable
being found only on the Rock Island of **Ngeruktabel** and
Peleliu. Good birding spots include **Ngeremdiu Beach** a
a long-abandoned stone dock and road through the forest
a lighthouse built by the Japanese on the eastern end of t
island. All of Palau's forest birds can be found here, includi
the rare Palau Ground Dove, although the dove is more eas
seen on **Ulong Island**, another good and accessible island
birding. **Carp Island** is a great spot for both waders and fore
birds. Nearly every beach on the Rock Islands has a meg
pode mound, and the birds are often seen and heard nearl
Rock Islands that are very tall with nearly vertical sides and f
tops are favored nesting sites for Tropical Shearwaters. T
best birding to be had in the Rock Islands, is by just drifti
along the inner lagoons in a boat with the engine off, listeni
to the forest chorus as pigeons, doves, terns and White-tail
Tropicbirds cruise overhead.

N

Rock Islands

Babeldaob

Koror

Ulong

Lighthouse channel

Milky
Way
Ngeruktabel

Ngeremdiu

Neco

Ngerukuid
70 Islands

Mecherchar-
Jellyfish Lake

Eil Malk

German
Channel

Denges passage

Ngerechong

elis

Ngercheu
/Carp

Peleliu

Peleliu and Angaur

At the southern end of the Rock Islands are two coral platfor
islands much flatter than the Rock Islands and suitable for lim
ited agriculture. Their forests are entirely secondary, becaus
the original forest was completely destroyed during one
World War II's bloodiest battles. The two islands are populate
by a few hundred people each, and both have regular sta
ferry boat service from Koror. Both Peleliu and Angaur hav
landing strips, and small planes used to fly here regularly, b
at the moment only chartered helicopter service is availabl
Basic accommodation and rental cars are available on bo
islands, and small stores sell drinks and canned food. Attra
tions on both islands include beautiful sandy beaches, rock
shores with spectacular blowholes at high tide, and World W
II artifacts.

When birding on Peleliu, watch out for aggressive dogs nea
the village, and do not stray away from the main road/ trail
since there are still a lot of unstable World War II explosive
and shells lying around in the jungle. Giant White-eyes can b
seen along the roads in the low **bedel** trees *Macaranga car
linensis*, the birds are named after this tree in Palauan. Th
freshwater ponds on both islands attract rare migratory wate
fowl, and shorebirds can be seen around the landing strip
The Little Pied Cormorant is abundant around Peleliu, ar
nests in the dense mangrove coastal areas. The flats aroun
the northern harbor entrance are good at low tide for spottir
shorebirds, egrets and herons.

South of Peleliu, Angaur is outside the protective reef that su
rounds all other islands except Kayangel. Angaur has a sma
freshwater lake formed by phosphate mining in the past, whe
you can spot the Common Moorhen, and it is one of the la
places in Palau where Pacific Black Ducks were seen. The
are several look-out points from the road over the lake, but
is difficult to get near the water, since the edges of the lake a
densely overgrown, and there are saltwater crocodiles in th
area. Birds in general are much reduced in numbers on Anga
because of egg predation by Indian monitor lizards *Varanus i
dicus* and long-tailed macaque monkeys *Macaca fascicular
both shown on the next page. The monkeys are descendan
of German pets brought to Palau a hundred years ago, a
they have had no trouble adapting to life in the wild here. E
forts are being made to control the monkeys and prevent the
further spread to other islands, but escaped pet monkeys livi
in the wild have been spotted on Koror and Babeldaob alread
Angaur is also the only island that has the Asian musk shre
Suncus murinus, aside from the four common rat speci
which are found on all the islands. Buff-banded Rails are s
fairly common on Angaur and can often be seen crossing t
dirt roads.

Ngedebus

Peleliu

Patrick L.Colin

Angaur

Patrick L.Colin

The Southwest Islands

To the southwest of the main Palau Islands lies a scatte
group of 6 tiny coral sand islands, which make up 2 of
16 states of Palau. Hatohobei state consists of Tobi Isla
and Helen Reef atoll, while Sonsorol consists of the islar
of Merir, Pulo Anna, Sonsorol and nearby Fana. Fewer th
100 people live here now, most on the islands of Hatoho
(Tobi), Pulo Anna and Sonsorol. Around 1904 there were o
a thousand people, mostly on Tobi. The first settlers origina
came from Yap, and the people here still speak a Yapese la
guage. They subsisted primarily on copra production and fis
ing. After a typhoon devastated the islands in 1904, survive
were relocated to Koror in 1906 by the German administ
tion. Of those left behind on Hatohobei, another 200+ d
from an epidemic after contact with a German ship in 19
Many Southwest islanders today still live in the village Echa
on Arakebesang, Koror. After 1906, Pulo Anna and Merir we
uninhabited for many years.

Ecologically, the Southwest Islands are also very differe
from the rest of Palau, with far fewer tree species prese
In fact, single-species forests of tree heliotrope *Tournefor
argentea* or *Pisonia grandis* grow in several places. Fa
Island, which is an official wildlife reserve, and Palau's fi
designated IBA (Important Bird Area), has one of the best c
veloped examples of *Pisonia* forest in the Pacific. Because t
islands of Fana and Helen have few visitors, they are imp
tant breeding grounds for seabirds. Two species of booby
frigatebirds, 2 tropicbirds, 2 noddies, Swift Terns, Fairy Ter
and Sooty Terns nest in abundance, although not all on a
one island. Merir and Helen are important Green turtle nesti
sites also.

Visiting these islands is a daunting prospect, but a real adve
ture. Best time to visit is between March and July, when t
weather is usually calm, and the green sea turtles *Chelor
mydas* as well as almost all the species of seabirds there a
mating and nesting. The government patrol boat and Sta
boat from Koror visit with unpredictable schedules, and son
times take visitors along, but there are no facilities for visito
on the islands. Another possibility is joining or chartering a t
on one of the live-aboard dive vessels from Koror, but this
costly, and as of this writing there are no regular trips offer
yet. All of this is probably a good thing, because it reduc
disturbance of the seabird colonies and lessens the chanc
for alien species to be introduced. If you do get the chan
to go, bring all your own supplies and waterproof bags
any camea gear. Extra drinking water is essential, as are re
boots and quick-dry clothes and towels. Be prepared for t
unexpected !

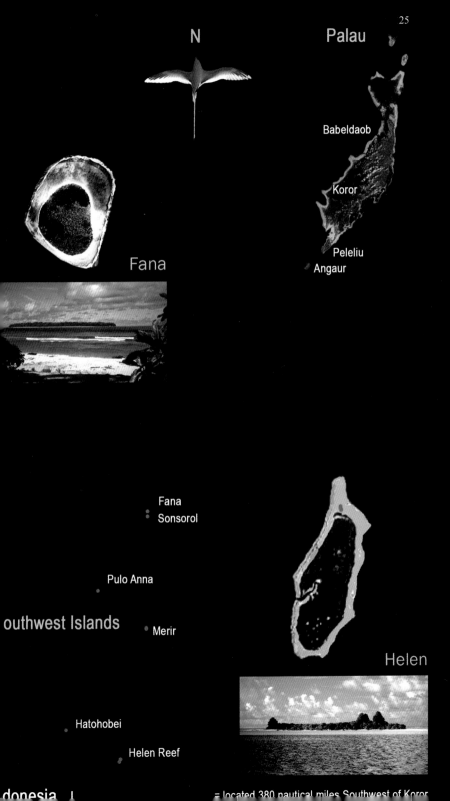

N

Palau

Babeldaob

Koror

Peleliu

Angaur

Fana

Fana
Sonsorol

Pulo Anna

outhwest Islands

Merir

Helen

Hatohobei

Helen Reef

donesia

= located 380 nautical miles Southwest of Koror

PALAU'S ENDEMIC BIRDS

Palau Fantail

Palau Swiftlet

Dusky White-eye

♂

Palau Bush Warbler

Palau Flycatcher

♀

Giant White-eye

Rusty-capped Kingfisher

Morningbird

♂

Palau Owl

Palau Cicadabird

♀

au Ground Dove

Palau Fruit Dove

BIRD NAMES AND CLASSIFICATION

In this book, birds can have up to 3 names: English, *Palauan*, and *scientific*. Palauan names are tradi-tional and straightforward, but English names have undergone a lot of changes recently in an effort standardize them worldwide. For a long time, some widespread species had different English name in Britain, North America and Australia, and arriving at a consensus has proven to be a challeng HDP worked on the committee of the International Ornithological Congress that produced *Birds the World: Recommended English Names* (Gill and Wright 2006) and agreed to use those names future publications. We use them herein (with one exception, see below) but give alternate names the text to avoid confusion. We are using American spelling for all names (e.g. Gray instead of Gre color instead of colour) because that is what we are used to and what is most familiar to Englis speaking Palauans. The IOC list does not consider alternative spellings to be different names. Als we are using some localized English names for Palauan subspecies that are likely to be considere species in the near future. The exception mentioned above is Angel Tern, coined by some membe of the IOC committee for *Gygis alba*, which is known almost universally among non-ornithologists the Fairy Tern. Because HDP and other believe there are actually 3 species included in the "Ang Tern", we have taken the liberty of returning to Fairy Tern as a group name, inasmuch as Angel Te has not yet gained widespread favor. This change will require that the bird known as Fairy Tern the IOC list, *Sterna nereis*, be modified, and we suggest Austral Fairy Tern, notwithstanding the fa that it is in another genus.

The scientific names of birds are in classical Latin, and always in italics. The first word in the name the **genus**, which is always capitalized. A **genus** may contain more than one species, and the sp cies are designated by the second part of the name, which is never capitalized. **Species** names a almost never written without the genus name or its initial (e.g. G. alba). Sometimes a name has a thi part, which designates it as a **subspecies**, also always lower case. Not all species have subspecie those that do not are called monotypic. Subspecies are geographically designated populations th differ enough to be distinguishable from other populations of the same species, but whose diffe ences are deemed insufficient to prevent interbreeding should the populations come into contact. the past, many island populations were classified as subspecies that probably are better regarde as full species, especially those that are well isolated with no potential for ever merging again wi their ancestral gene pool. Several Palau endemics fall into this catagory, but we have chosen classify them as subspecies pending publication in a peer-reviewed journal of the rationale for givir them species status (HDP is preparing such a publication simultaneously with this book). Howeve we are using distinctive English names for them to indicate their pending status. For example, th Rusty-capped Kingfisher is currently regarded as a subspecies of the Micronesian Kingfisher, whic has other subspecies on Guam and Pohnpei. These three populations look very different, and mo importantly have very different nesting habits, such that they probably could not interbreed succes fully even if they had the opportunity. So we give it the scientific name *Halcyon cinnamomina pele ensis*, but fully expect that it will soon be just *Halcyon pelewensis*. When subspecies are recogniz as species, the third name moves up to the second position, and there is no third name. Others this category are the Palau Megapode, Palau Woodswallow, and Palau Cicadabird.

Birds are also grouped into higher categories above the genus. The most important in this book is t **family**. Bird family names bear the suffix -idae, and are based on the genus with the oldest nam Families are grouped into orders, which always end in -iformes. The main **order** of concern herein the Passeriformes, which contains about half of the world's bird species. Members of this order a called **passerines**, while members of all other orders are often grouped as **nonpasserines**. Pa serines are the familiar birds we call perching birds or songbirds.

BIRD TOPOGRAPHY

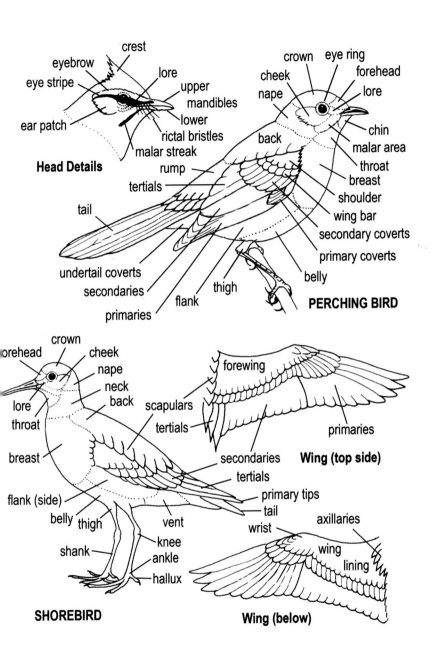

Head Details

crest
eyebrow
eye stripe
lore
upper
mandibles
lower
rictal bristles
malar streak
ear patch

crown eye ring
cheek
nape
forehead
lore
chin
malar area
throat
breast
shoulder
wing bar
secondary coverts
primary coverts
belly

back
rump
tertials
tail
undertail coverts
secondaries
primaries
flank
thigh

PERCHING BIRD

crown
forehead
cheek
nape
neck
back
scapulars
tertials
lore
throat
breast
flank (side)
belly thigh
shank
vent
knee
ankle
hallux

SHOREBIRD

forewing
primaries

Wing (top side)

secondaries
tertials
primary tips
tail
wrist
axillaries
wing
lining

Wing (below)

The traditional drawings/ carvings shown on these page were copied from Palauan **Bai**, traditional meeting hous es, by the German anthropologist Augustin Kramer du ing his visits in 1908-1910. Most of these buildings we destroyed afterwards by typhoons and during World W II, when Palauans were forced to move away from th villages. Palauans have many old stories and legends volving birds and bats.

The beautiful long tail streamers of the White-tailed Tro icbird *Phaethon lepturus* **dudek**, were traditionally ma into a comb, and are still used to decorate the hair of P lauan women during their 1st Childbirth Ceremony. Only few select families are allowed to use this particular dec ration, depending on the mothers' clan. Other clans wis ing to use it, must ask for permission. The tropicbird wa and occasionally still is, taken for food by Palauans.

The Tropical Shearwater *Puffinus bailloni* **ochaieu** is a t ditional god in the State of Ngchesar on Babeldaob Islan along with the spotted eagle ray *Aetobatis narinari*, whi shares the same local name. The bird is depicted on th State flag. Both animals are protected by law and custo and even today Palauans are very superstituous abc harming this bird. It is said a relative will be hurt or die someone in a Ngchesar family clan harms a shearwater eagle ray, even if by accident.

The large eggs of the Palau *Megapode Megapodius perouse senex* **bekai** are considered a delicacy in P lau, but the bird itself is not hunted or eaten. The lege shown below tells of and old woman who kept a turtle a a megapode as pets. One day when she was out in h taro patches, the birds made a nest in the hot ashes of h cooking fire, so that the heat could incubate their egg The woman got angry at the mess they had made, a chased the animals out. The turtle swam off to the Rc Islands with the megapode on its back, and ever after t turtle had to lay its eggs in the sand of the beaches the heat will incubate its eggs, and the megapode lays eggs in the soil of the forest for the same reason.

e Whimbrel *Numenius phaeopus* **okak**, a winter migrant
Palau, is also called the Palauan moneybird, or **delaroch**,
bird that according to legend brought the first glass mon-
beads to Palau. It is often depicted as a stylized paint-
on the four corner extensions of the window ledges of
raditional **bai** meeting house, with beads coming out of
bill and body. Some believe the bird signifies that the
ads were brought in from overseas, just like the **okak** flies
Palau every winter from other countries. The circle with
cross in it stands for wealth and money. The moneybird
mbol is also shown on the State flag of Melekeok State
Babeldaob.

e photo showing a traditional moneybird symbol at right is
m the only original **bai** remaining on Palau in Airai State,
ich was built in the 1890s. Traditional paint was made us-
clay and oil from nuts, in earth-tone colors, and the out-
es of the painted symbols were carved in detail.

e Ngardmau State flag shows a Great Frigatebird *Fregata
nor* **kedam**. According to legend the land in that state was
med when a frigatebird swooped down from the sky, and
state is still formed in the shape of this magnificent bird.

rved statues of the Collared Kingfisher *Todiramphus chlo-
teraokai* **tengadidik** traditionally decorated both ends of
hull of the **kaeb**, Palau's fastest racing canoe, with a hull
aped like a half moon. The kingfisher was seen as a good
herman and hunter, and used as a good-luck charm, lead-
fishermen back to land. Elsewhere in the Pacific and Mi-
nesia the kingfisher was also often used as a carving or
mbol on traditional canoes. The photo shown here of the
atpang State **kaeb** canoe was taken during the 2004 Pa-
c Arts Festival which took place in Palau. These canoes
ve not been built or used in Palau for several decades.

According to the British sailors stranded on Palau in 17[...] Palauans ate the eggs of the Red Junglefowl *Gallus ga[...] malkureomel*, but not the bird itself, until the British s[...] ors showed them how to cook it and introduced the c[...] to the Chiefs. Cock fights, although illegal, are still popu[...] today in the villages. The rooster was a traditional des[...] used on the posts of the Palauan *bai* meeting hous[...] always on a black background. Palauans believed that [...] ancient scattered monoliths in Ngerchelong State m[...] have been the foundation of the first *bai* meeting hou[...] to be build by gods, who could only work during the nig[...] The crow of a rooster one early morning put an abrupt h[...] to the work, and the building was never completed.

Pigeons have always been a delicacy in Palau, and [...] cooked whole in a clear broth. Palauans used to h[...] them with blow guns and bow and arrow, using a hide a[...] a tied captive pigeon to lure the wild birds closer. Tod[...] although illegal, they are still being hunted with airgu[...] and served during special occasions.

A white Micronesian Imperial Pigeon *Ducula ocean[...] belochel* is depicted on the Peleliu State flag, based [...] a legend about the Neriab Pigeon that laid Palauan m[...] eyebeads instead of eggs.

The small Palau Fruit Dove *Ptilinopus pelewensis* b[...] and the giant clam *otkang* are featured in an old lege[...] about a beautiful Palauan girl from Ulong, and her moth[...] The girl was called Biib, and forced to marry a man s[...] did not love. The mother threatened to change into a cl[...] when the girl was running off in a canoe with her lov[...] According to the legend they both drowned. Palauans [...] never put a dead clam next to a captive fruit dove, beli[...] ing that the sound the bird makes is actually a mourn[...] for its dead mother.

ght: This detail of a painting by Palauan artist chucher Charlie Gibbons (1894 -1988) shows the traional hunting of the fruit bat *olik*. Palauans would built platform high in the trees and catch the bats at night h a triangular net fastened to a long bamboo pole, led *sigero*. Fruit bats are still occasionally eaten by lauans today and served in some local and Japanese staurants, cooked whole in a clear broth. (*Original inting owned by Greg and Maura Gordon, displayed the Etpison Museum*).

e main entrance beams to a traditional *bai* meetinguse always have paintings of three flying fruit bats erhead as one enters. These refer to the legend of a ant fruit bat from Babeldaob. The bat flew to Angaur, d destroyed their bai. The monster bat terrorized the ople there until they found a way to lure it close, using eet almonds and grated coconut. When swooping wn to get the sweets, the huge bat impaled itself on e sharp spears the warriors had put on top of their Bai.

low, right: In 1899 this Palauan inlaid pot in the shape a duck was donated to the Museum fur Volkerkunde in esden, Germany, by an early collector. Below, left: In 83 this wooden inlaid pot, shaped like the Palau egapode, was given to Captain Wilson of the British p Antelope by Chief Ibedul of Koror. Today it is still in e British Museum Collection. These intricate wooden ssels were carved with a simple shell blade adze, aid with white shells, and varnished with oil squeezed m the meat of a local *Parinarium* nut called *cheritm*. ey were owned by the highest chiefs and used to rve sweet drinks during village feasts. These are the ly two of their kind known today, and they are not ing made anymore. All big rounded clay pots are led *bekai* in Palauan, after the megapode bird.

BIRDS ON PALAU POSTAGE STAM

Stamp collecting is one of the world's most popular hobbie: many nations produce postage stamps with the collector, a as postal needs, in mind. Palau is no exception. When first became postally independent in the early 1980s, the Postal Service contracted the Inter-Governmental Philateli poration (IGPC) of New York to handle its stamp program. found HDP, who not only knew Palau's birds firsthand, bu an experienced illustrator and collector of bird stamps hi He was hired to design Palau's first bird-themed stamps. of four endemics (below right), became the second set issu the new postal entity. For several years, HDP continued t duce designs for Palau, eventually depicting the entire re avifauna plus many migratory visitors. He always insisted th stamps show only Palauan species. Stamps designed by are shown throughout this book, thanks to the generous pe sion of the Palau Postal Service. The stamps were usually i in blocks of 4 designs, with some unifying theme. In one exa shown on the facing page, the entire sheet of stamps was gle design, depicting birds over the Palau lagoon, but eac was also the subject of a single stamp. Such designs p obvious challenges to the artist with regard to perspectiv relative sizes of the birds, but help to put the birds into their ral habitats. As a result of changes at IGPC, other artists wit knowledge of Palau were hired to work on Palau stamps. sequent issues, though falsely labeled as birds/ flowers/ sh Palau, have shown African, Australian and Asian species th never seen in Palau. These issues were clearly aimed dire the collector market, but because they misrepresented the did a disservice to the educational value of stamps in F Recently, the postal service has returned to its earlier Pala cies-only policy, and the most recent bird stamps feature sc MTE's bird photographs.

Birds over the Palau Lagoon

glish names and scientific names of the birds depicted are, left-right, from the top down are:

BIRDING IN PALAU

Birding, as it has come to be known (the term birdwatching is now old-fashioned), is one of the world's most popular pastimes, and has even taken on the trappings of a competitive sport among some enthu siasts. Birders now travel the world in the pursuit of new species to add to their "life lists". In the species chase, remote oceanic islands take on a special significance because the larger ones nearly always have one or more endemic species. Islands do not produce huge lists of species such as one might find in the rainforests of Peru or Malaysia, but what they have to offer cannot be seen anywhere else. Also the majority of the world's endangered species are island birds because small islands are much more ecologically sensitive to outside disturbance than large islands or continents. Island endemics are in many ways the crown jewels of birding, and Palau has it's share. There is still much to be learned about Palau's birds, and non-professionals have a real opportunity to contribute to our knowledge with their observations and photographs.

Palau also provides birding excitement in the form of rare migrants. Thus local birders need never tire of looking, even though they routinely see the endemics, because there is the ever-present possibility of turning up a bird new to Palau, or even Micronesia. Such "scores" are just as exciting, if not more so, than adding a species to one's personal list. The Palau list includes a great many "one-record wonders", including such unexpected things as Australian Pelican, Brahminy Kite, Red- kneed Dotterel, Chestnut-winged Cuckoo, Brush Cuckoo, Narcissus Flycatcher, and Chestnut-cheeked Starling, to mention just a few. In fact, almost any bird that migrates from eastern Asia to the Philippines or Indonesia, or from Aus tralia to New Guinea, could turn up in Palau. As recently as 2006, MTE photographed a Scaly Trush at Palau for the first Micronesia record. Some birds, such as Whiskered tern, Blue Rock Thrush, and Gray-streaked Flycatcher, once thought to be vagrants, have turned out, thanks to reports by birders, to be rare but regular visitors.

So, armed with insect repellent, sunblock, and binoculars or camera, you will find Palau a marvelous place to bird. Unlike other tropical areas, Palau has no poisonous or dangerous wildlife, aside from a rarely seen centipede, lurking in its forests. Mosquitoes, though annoying, are less troublesome here than in many places, and carry no malaria, although there are occasional dengue fever outbreaks. The few small land snakes are harmless, and although the poisonous sea krait comes out of the water to rest it is docile and poses no threat. Saltwater crocodiles are present but shy, mostly nocturnal, and live pri marily deep in mangrove forests where birders rarely go. However, a few hazards do exist, and birders should be aware of:

- ✔ Chiggers, mainly in the Rock Islands. Always coat your legs and feet with repellent if you go into the woods behind a beach. Decaying palm fronds on the ground often harbor these pests which cause red itching bumps, and can stay on your skin for days. Soaking in salt water for about an hour and dipping alcohol on the bites helps remove the tiny red bugs.

- ✔ No-see-ums (tiny biting flies that make painful bites and are small enough to penetrate mos quito netting), fly mostly from dusk into the night. Large biting flies are out during the day on certain beaches. They are sluggish, are strangely attracted to anything colored blue, and are unfazed by repellent.

- ✔ Walking into spider webs can be very annoying and unpleasant. Watch for the huge orb webs of the hand-sized *Nephila* spiders (harmless). A stick held in front of you will help.

- ✔ Thorny vines, of which there are several species in the Palau forest.

- ✔ The Palau poison tree *Semecarpus venenosus* **tonget**, whose trunk and leaves produce a con tact poison similar in effect to poison ivy. Susceptibility varies, but you should avoid touching this tree, and the long blade-like leaves, which are broader at the tip than at the base. The leaves grow in rosettes at the end of branches. The trunk exudes a characteristic black sap.

ling sites on Babeldaob and the Koror Complex can be
ched by car, and rentals are readily available. Note, how-
r, that some places on Babeldaob may require 4-wheel
e, depending on recent weather conditions. But to really
erience Palau at its birding best, a boat is essential. Many
and dive operators offer boats for hire either as regular or-
ized tours, or charters. One can also rent kayaks for ex-
ing the Rock Islands, but waterproof containers for gear is
ust. Boats among the Rock Islands are well run and com-
able, and the lagoon waters are usually quite calm. On any
it, you should carry protective coverings for binoculars and
nera equipment, and lens cloths for removing the inevitable
spray. In addition to the absolutely essential binoculars, a
tting scope with sturdy tripod is a very useful tool for the
ler in Palau, particularly for identifying distant shorebirds, or
n for close ones that require detailed examination for posi-
identifications. Of course, a scope is not usable in a
ving boat.

to the boat driver or guide ahead of time, so he knows
at you are looking for, and ask him to go slow and close
und the islands so you can spot birds. Birding is a new
g in Palau, and the boats normally zoom through the is-
ds at full speed. Most local boat drivers grew up hunting
ls, and once they understand what you are looking for, can
you valuable tips on where to find the birds you are look-
for, and in what trees they can be found. Always check the
tables before going out on a boat, since Palau's tide
anges can be extreme, and will affect which islands/ beach-
you will be able to go to, and where the best spots for
ders will be on that day at low tide.

visits to Peleliu, Angaur, or Kayangel, you will need to
arter a boat, helicopter, or join the state ferry boats. There
several small hotels to stay overnight on Peleliu and
gaur, but none on Kayangel. You can make arrangements
advance to stay with a local family or ask permission to
np if you have your own gear. Small stores sell drinks and
ned food on all three islands, but you have to remember
se islands are not as developed as Koror. When visiting
se islands or the much more remote Southwest Islands, it
always a good idea to call their state offices on Koror first to
d out the latest on permits, fees, schedules and available
commodations, or ask your travel agent to get this informa-
n for you ahead of time, since these things tend to change
m time to time.

Aside from birding, there are many things here to d▮
nature lovers. Palau's reefs are famous among scuba d▮
and snorkelers for the steep drop-offs with large scho▮
fish and resident gray reef sharks. WWII ship wr▮
mantas and Giant clams can be seen also, and a visit t▮
lyfish Lake (left), where you can swim with thousands o▮
stinging jellies, is a must for all tourists.

Good birders keep notes and records of what they see▮
just to cherish the memories, but because, in the purs▮
their hobby, they can make important contributions to the▮
ence of ornithology. If you see a bird in Palau that is r▮
this book, you should make careful notes about identific▮
details, date, locality; or better still, get a recognizable p▮
graph. Then, send your information to someone who▮
make it known to the scientific community. Unfortun▮
that is not as easy as it sounds for a place like Palau, v▮
has no resident ornithologist, and which does not fall u▮
the jurisdiction of any large continental ornithological or▮
zation such as the American Ornithologists' Union (AO▮
the Royal Autralasian Ornithologists' Union (RAOU)▮
cover some of the other islands in the tropical Pacific.▮
authors of this book are happy to receive any such re▮
(see addresses and emails in Preface), as is the Palau ▮
servation Society. Although it is not the job of PCS to ▮
track of bird records, they are happy to forward them to c▮
fied ornithologists. The journals *Micronesica*, publishe▮
the University of Guam, and *Elepaio*, from the Hawaii A▮
bon Society, continue to be the main venues for publis▮
important bird sightings from Palau, but a number of c▮
scientific journals do so as well.

SYMBOLS USED IN THE SPECIES ACCOUN▮

E Endangered; may be designated as such by Pala▮
U.S.statute, BirdLife International, or a combina▮

C Conservation concern; equivalent to the "Near Th▮
ened" catagory of BirdLife International.

E Endemic species.

e Endemic subspecies.

I Indigenous resident species

A Alien species introduced to Palau

M Migratory species that pass through Palau e▮
year August - November and March - May. A few ▮
remain through the northern winter season.

W Migratory visitors that spend the northern winte▮
Palau, but may be augmented by passage migran▮
the same species in spring and fall.

V Visitor found irregularly and unpredictably.

Bert Yates

Bert Yates

BIRDS OF FORESTS, OPEN COUNTRY, AND VILLAGES

Terrestrial habitats are the most bird-rich in Palau, and harbor all of the endemic species. Whereas seabirds, shorebirds, and freshwater birds tend to belong to widespread species, many of which are migratory, Palau's land birds are mostly year-round residents. The land bird community is often divided into two groups, the nonpasserines such as megapodes, pigeons and doves, rails, swifts, owls, kingfishers, and cuckoos, and passerines. Passerines belong to the largest order of birds, Passeriformes, and are commonly known as perching birds or songbirds. Endemic species are any island's "crown jewels" as far as birders are concerned, and Palau is blessed with a large number of them. Most of the endemics are forest dwellers, because most of Palau was covered with forest before the coming of humans. An exception is the woodswallow, which has adapted to savannas rather than deep forests, and thus has a restricted distribution. Many of the forest birds have proven adaptable to habitat changes, and can be found in introduced trees and secondary forest as well as primary forests. Many of them can be seen close to houses in towns and villages. With a few notable exceptions, Palau's endemics are easily observed without venturing far from one's home or hotel. A few land birds regularly spend their winters in Palau, or pass through on migration, but nest elsewhere. Palau is not far off the main migration route for birds that nest in eastern Asia but winter from the Philippines to New Guinea, and often a few stray from the path and turn up here. A few, such as the Eastern Yellow Wagtail, are present in good numbers every year. Palau also sometimes receives migratory birds from Australia that overshoot their normal destinations to the south. In addition to its endemics and migratory visitors, Palau has a few alien species that were introduced, either by accident or on purpose, by people. These include two parrots that have become serious ecological pests, and show why placing a species in a new location is a bad idea.

Official First Day Cover

FOREST BIRDS
1990

Daphne Gemmill

Shallum Etpison

PALAU MEGAPODE/ BEKAI
Megapodius laperouse senex

E

Megapodiid

L 38 cm, 15 in. The Palau Megapode is a ground-dwelling chicken-like bird most often seen near bea¢ es. It has a dark gray, nearly black, body and bright golden yellow legs and bill. The feathers on the ne and sides of the head are thin, allowing the bright red skin to show through, and a tuft of paler gray fea ers adorn the back of the head. As the name megapode (from Latin for "big foot") implies, the feet are c proportionately large. Megapodes are smaller than domestic chickens, but still among the larger w birds at Palau.

Megapodes are often quite shy, and run away when approached, although they can fly well. They c become tame in places where they see many people if they are not harassed. They reveal their presen with their loud *skeek* calls, and when a pair are foraging together, they keep in contact by performing duet. The male gives a series of *keeks* that build to a 3-note *keek-keeer-kew*, with the middle n¢ downslurred, and the female immediately adds a low chuckle that slows as it rises in intensity and pi¹ to end in an emphatic single note: *kukukuku-ku-kuh-kuh-kuh-kuh-KUCK*! Both males and females m also call without duetting.

Megapodes have unusual nesting habits. They lay their large white egg in large communal mounds sand, rubble, and vegetation raked up using their huge feet. The mounds may be up to 2m high and a often placed at the base of a large dead tree. In the deep forest, they may be made up entirely of leav and other vegetable matter. As the organic matter decays, it produces heat that incubates the eggs.

Most mounds are in shady spots, so the sun doe~ contribute much to the process. The adult ~ check the mounds regularly to make sure the ~ perature is right, and make adjustments by ope~ up the mound for air to circulate if it's too hot, or ~ on more insulation if too cool. But when it com~ caring for the young, these are hardly model ~ ents... When the eggs hatch, the chicks have t~ their way out of the mound on their own, and ~ begin foraging for food immediately without any ~ from the parents. Food for megapodes can be ~ about anything from seeds and nuts to crabs ar~ sects. They search for tidbits by kicking leaf ~ around with their big feet. Newly hatched chicks ~ nothing like adults, but are just little brown ba~ feathers mottled with orange spots. As they ~ they gradually take on the taller posture, d~ plumage, and colorful skin of adulthood.

Although they are widely distributed and easy t~ in some places, Palau Megapodes are listed as ~ dangered because their habitat, especially p~ sites for nest mounds, is limited and subject to a ~ disturbance. The birds themselves are not hunt~ Palau, but the large eggs are a traditional delicac~ Palauans.

t mounds are still regularly raided, eventhough it
gainst the law to do so. Other enemies include
itor lizards, rats, and feral cats, so they do better
slands free of these pests, and are rarely found
e days on the larger inhabited islands like Koror
Babeldaob. Probably to avoid predators, mega-
es roost in the low branches of trees, often
nst a coral cliff. The sleeping birds hide their
and feet completely within their feathers.

apodes are members of a group called gallina-
us (chicken-like) birds that also includes pheas-
, partridges and domestic chickens. But unlike
relatives, which almost never reach isolated is-
s without the help of people, megapodes are
d island colonizers and are found on many
ote islands of the Indo-Pacific Region. The
u Megapode is currently considered a subspe-
along with a relative in the Mariana Islands, of
Micronesian Megapode, but vocal and ecologi-
differences indicate the two may actually be dif-
nt species.

RED JUNGLEFOWL/ MALKUREOMEL
Gallus gallus   Phasiani◄

L male 76 cm, 30 in; female 43 cm, 17 in. This unmistakable descendant of domestic chickens was the bird brought to Palau by humans. The original Red Junglefowl is found in India, and is the ancestor of many varieties of chickens we know today. On many Pacific islands including Palau, birds have esca into the forest and reverted to a wild state, and often have come to closely resemble their wild ancest They show much less variation than farm-raised chickens, and the chicks have stripes on their head like wild junglefowl. The roosters often have a tuft of fluffy white feathers at the base of the tail, and b hens and roosters may have darker legs than domestic ones. However, they still can and do interbr with farm chickens, fighting cocks, or pets, so some domestic genes constantly creep into the wild pop tion.

Junglefowl are most often found in forests near villages, and are common on Angaur and Peleliu. T prefer more level areas than are found in most of the limestone islands, so they are scarce there, altho on beaches where people have attempted to live, the descendants of their chickens can be seen forag with Palau Megapodes. The two do not seem to compete, and they are, in fact, distant cousins. rooster's familiar dawn crow is a surprising sound when one is far from any human habitation.

Wild Red Junglefowl live more or less the same way as domestic birds, foraging on the ground for w ever is available. Hens with broods of chicks are entertaining to watch as the mother demonstrates fo ing techniques for the young to mimic. One might suppose that the wild birds would be hunted, but in they are usually not pursued by hunters, partly because wild birds tend to be tough and scrawny compa to farm-raised chickens. They do have enemies, however, including rats and monitor lizards that may nests, and feral cats that take chicks.

H. Douglas Pratt

RAPTORS

Birds of prey, often called raptors, are seldom seen in Palau. No species nests here, and those that do so in very low numbers. Nevertheless, every year a few hawks, ospreys, or falcons are seen an the islands. The Chinese Sparrowhawk is probably present every year in low numbers, but the other irregular and unpredictable. The ones discussed on this page include those species seen most rec Female raptors are noticably larger than males of the same species.

Eric VanderWerf

BLACK KITE ↖

Milvus migrans　　　　　　　Accipitr

L m. 58 cm, 23 in; f. 68 cm, 27 in. Although it is one c world's most numerous and widespread raptors, this cies has only recently expanded its range into the tro Pacific and is still only an occasional visitor to Palau. distinctive in having long narrow wings with pale pat at the base of the primaries and a broad tail that is s lowly notched in the center. It eats all kinds of small mals, but is also a scavenger.

Eric VanderWerf

PEREGRINE FALCON

Falco peregrinus　　　　　　Falcon

L m.41 cm, 51 in; f. 51 cm, 20 in. Falcons are distinguis among raptors by their long pointed wings, narrow and powerful flight. The Peregrine Falcon is fc throughout the world, but is only a rare visitor in Micr sia. They are almost entirely bird hunters, taking their in steep dives that make them the world's fastest bird

Thomas Dove

OSPREY

Pandion haliaetus　　　　　　Accipitri

L .55 cm, 22 in; f. 64 cm, 25 in. The cosmopolitan Os is a rare visitor to Palau, and the largest raptor reco here. It is easily recognized by its eagle-like profile w characteristic kink in the wings, and dark above/ v below color pattern. Its head is white with a dark eyest Ospreys feed on fish they catch by plunging into the w feet first.

HINESE SPARROWHAWK M

ipiter soloensis   Accipitridae

. 31 cm, 12 in; f. 35 cm, 14 in. Accipiters characteristi-
y have short rounded wings and long square-tipped
. This one breeds in China and Korea, and winters
h to Indonesia. A few individuals stray every year to
au, where it is the most commonly seen raptor, often
ring over lagoon waters among the Rock Islands in
ober/ November. Adults, as shown here, are sleek
above and beige below, but younger birds show
ing in the wing and tail feathers, and streaks below.
y eat any small birds or animals they can catch, and
ally hunt from a perch.

Michelle & Peter Wong

RAHMINY KITE V

iastur indus   Accipitridae

. 51 cm, 20 in; f. 43 cm, 17 in. This striking rufous and
e kite is common from India to Australia, but has
n seen only once at Palau. John Kochi reported a
in the Ngeruluid Islands in the 1970s. It is often seen
ring over coastal areas.

Jacob Faust

RAY-FACED BUZZARD V

astur indicus   Accipitridae

. 51 cm, 20 in; f. 47 cm, 18.5 in. This small raptor, with
er long narrow wings and a black line down the
dle of the throat, has recently turned up at several
es in western Micronesia, including Palau. The indi-
al shown was found injured on Yap, rehabilitated and
ased by naturalist Marjorie Falanruw. Gray-faced
zards eat mainly frogs, lizards and large insects that
hunt from a stationary perch.

Marjorie Falanruw

SLATY-LEGGED CRAKE/ ULERRATEL, KOK, OCH
Rallina eurizonoides   Rallic

L 25 cm, 10 in. Most members of the rail family live in wetlands such as marshes and taro patches,
this exceptional species is a bird of the forest floor. It is shy, secretive, and mostly nocturnal, so m
people have never seen one, even where they are relatively common, as in the forests of the Koror cc
plex. In fact, until recently, the bird was thought to be only a migratory visitor to Palau because ea
naturalists had missed it! Robert P.Owen, who was the conservation officer for the old Trust Territor
the Pacific Islands, of which Palau was a part, confirmed that this bird, formerly sometimes called
Banded Crake, was a Palau resident when he saw a mother with chicks on Koror in the early 1970s
about the same time, HDP recorded a nocturnal vocalization that turned out to be this species.

Learning the voice was a big help in determining the status of this bird, because the bird is much m
easily heard than seen, learning the voice was key to determining its status. The song is a monoton
ow-ow-ow... heard most often at night, but also at dawn and dusk and sometimes during the day wl
the weather is cloudy and humid. The call may be just a single note, which is probably the basis of
bird's two shorter Palauan names. We now know, based mostly on voice observations, that the Sla
legged Crake is found from Babeldaob to Angaur, including the Rock islands, often close to villages. C
side Palau, this species ranges from India to the Philippines and Sulawesi.

When calling at night, the bird usually perches in thick vegetation, such as a bamboo thicket, but du
daylight it may vocalize on the ground. But hearing this crake and seeing it are two different things! H
has been within a meter of a calling bird without being able to catch a glimpse! On occasion, though, t
seem less shy. Visiting birders have reported them bathing in the open in roadside rain pools at the Pa
Pacific Resort. One way to try to see one is to sit by a forest puddle at dusk in an area where the b
have been heard calling and hope one comes in to bathe. A flashlight is handy, and doesn't seem
frighten the bather. All photos shown here by MTE were taken on Koror.

Getting a look at this striking bird is well worth the effort. In a family of rather dull-colored species, this c
is a beauty, with a rufous-chestnut head and breast, brown back, and black-and-white barred underpa▪
But the most impressive feature is undoubtedly the large bright red eye, surrounded by a yellow fles
eye ring. The eye is large to enable the bird to see in very low light. The bill is a beautiful pearly li▪
green, with blue overtones. The bird walks with a jerky gait, often flicking its tail, which is held up at
angle. It is unfortunate that such a handsome bird is so hard to see... A very similar species, the **Re
legged Crake** *Rallina fasciata* was found at Palau in the 1800s, but has not been reported since. It diff▪
in having bright red legs and barring on the wings, and in being more of a wetland bird. It was appare▪
a migratory visitor, so it could turn up again.

Nothing was known about the nesting habits of the Slaty-legged Crake at Palau until MTE discovere▪
nest near her house on eastern Koror, in a brushy area that was being cleared for farming. The nest w▪
a bulky platform of leaves and sticks, similar to nests that have been reported elsewhere. It was plac
about a meter above the ground in a clump of *Pandanus*. In the central depression two glossy white eg
were being incubated. Both parents are thought to participate in incubation and raising the young. T
nest was exposed by the land clearing operations and could not be followed through the breeding cyc
The downy chicks are all black with relatively huge feet and are believed to take 3-4 weeks to beco▪
fully feathered. They can run very soon after they hatch. The juvenile plumage is like a dull, washed-▪
version of the adult without any chestnut and lacking the bright eye and bill colors.

PALAU GROUND DOVE/ OMEKRENGUKL, DOLDOL

Gallicolumba canifrons

C

Columbida

L 22 cm, 8.5 in. This is Palau's rarest endemic bird. Many Palauans are completely unfamiliar with it, ar birding visitors miss it more than any other species. The difficulty comes not only from the low numbe of birds, but from their quiet and retiring habits and distribution among relatively inaccessible island Nevertheless, the Palau Ground Dove is not on the verge of extinction, and the persistent observer c usually find it.

Until recently, only one plumage of Palau Ground Dove was known. It is certainly that of the adult mal but we don't know whether females look the same because the relatively few specimens in museums a almost all males. Birds in this plumage have a reddish brown back, black belly, and pale pearly gray hea and chest, the latter tinged with pink and sharply divided from the dark belly. The hindneck and upp back display a patch of bright rufous, and a flash of similar color shows in the base of the primaries whe the bird flies. The shoulders are adorned with bright maroon-purple. A somewhat duller plumage is simil in pattern, but with the gray much darker and fading into a dark brown belly without a sharp color brea the purple on the shoulder much reduced or absent, and the back tinged with olive green. Ornithologis are still trying to determine whether such birds are adult females or immatures of either sex. Recentl birds in this dull plumage were seen behaving like adult females in courtship encounters, but others hav been observed that seem to be molting from this plumage to the brighter one. An all rusty brown plumag paler where the adult male is gray, and known only from observations and a single specimen, could re resent the juvenile plumage or a rare variant form. Much remains to be learned about these color pa terns. Photos taken at the Rock Islands of Ngeremdiu and Ulong.

Ground Doves were once found throughout the archipelago from Babeldaob to Angaur, but were alw
rare on the former. Recently, they have declined drastically on Angaur, according to local observers,
MTE could not find any there on recent visits. They seem to prefer the limestone islands, where they
run over the rough substrate with remarkable ease. They fly only when pursued or startled, and then
into the air with a clap of wings, fly a short distance, and drop into a hiding place. They forage for se
and other foods in flatter areas such as beaches and ravines where leaf litter accumulates, and see
like areas densely overgrown with ferns. These are the same areas preferred by Palau Megapodes,
the two are often found together.

Unlike the highly vocal fruit doves, Palau Ground Doves are silent most of the time. Their territorial s
is a long series of low notes given a little less than 1 per second, each one with a rising inflection; c
oooa oooa etc. It is rarely heard any time other than dawn or dusk, and is usually given from the sa
song perch day after day. Occasionally, foraging birds may utter a different call, a low moan very simila
the moan of the Micronesian Imperial Pigeon but quieter. Ground doves roost high off the ground in tre
and have been observed as high as 8-9 m. Perhaps this is a defense against tree-climbing rats.

What little is known about the breeding habits of Palau Ground Doves comes second-hand from local
servers. Two reported nests were simple stick platforms in tree crotches, about 1 m off the ground.
found on Angaur was said to hold 3 white eggs, which would have been an extraordinary number fo
island ground dove, so the possibility that these nests were misidentified by Palauans must be conside
Often, nests are discovered accidentally when clearing for farming, and then destroyed by predator
abandoned before naturalists can examine them. Nests have been reported in September only.

PALAU FRUIT DOVE / BIIB
Ptilinopus pelewensis   Columbi¤

L 23 cm, 9 in. The lovely Palau Fruit Dove, or Biib, was chosen by local school children to be Palau's (
un-official) National Bird. It is common on the main islands, and its voice is one of the most character¤
sounds of the Palauan environment. It belongs to a group of small fruit-eating doves that are widespr¤
among the islands of the Pacific, but even in that colorful context, it stands out. Seeing one of these b¤
well takes some effort and stealth, because the birds are shy of approaching humans (probably with g¤
reason based on heavy hunting in the past).

Seen flying away, or across a road, the bird looks pale in the front with a green body and a bold ye¤
band at the tip of the fan-shaped tail. But when one finally does get a good look, the effort is rewar¤
immediately because this is a stunningly beautiful bird. The pale gray head and breast are accented ¤
crimson cap with a thin yellow border, orange-red eyes, and a yellow-green bill. The feathers in the ce¤
of the breast have a peculiar shape, as if the outer end has been cut away to leave a notched tip. Th¤
odd-shaped feathers are gray at the tip, but crimson at the base, and when they line up in rows, they f¤
grooves, like rows of arrow-shaped dots, that reveal the crimson base color. The center of the underp¤
shows a bright orange patch, bordered on each side by olive green. Behind that is a yellow band, and
undertail coverts are bright crimson-red. A close look at the dorsal side reveals iridescent blue centers ¤
yellow edges on the wing coverts. One might think that such gaudy colors would make this bird har¤
miss among the leaves, but just the opposite is the case. Because the colors are in big blocks that do
follow the contour of the bird itself, they break up the bird's shape so that instead of a bird, we see m¤
leaves (both fresh green and older yellow and red ones) and a spot of light coming through, and no bir¤
all! Scientists call this kind of camouflage "disruptive coloration".

One of the best ways to get a good look at a P
Fruit Dove is to sit quietly beneath a tree that has
of ripe fruit. The birds often congregate in fru
trees and may become so involved in their fee
that they allow one to make a close approach
get a great look. They eat all kinds of fruit, but
favorites are the small figs (*Ficus*) that grow ab
dantly in Palau's forests, and can be seen on or
the following pages. The dove swallows small f
whole, but larger ones are eaten in bites, and co
quently have to be very soft. While feeding, P
Fruit Doves may utter a quiet mooing or moa
sound, similar to a common call of the Microne
Imperial Pigeon, but much quieter.

One way NOT to get a good look at a fruit dove
try to follow its voice. Though loud and far carry
the hooting "song" has an echoing quality that ma
it sound farther away than it is, so a stalker often
too close before realizing it, and the bird flies a
The voice also is hard to locate because a single
can sound like it is in two different places just by t
ing on its perch. The ornithological term for such
leading vocalizations is "ventriloquial." The r
song of the Palau Fruit Dove is a long series of h
that begin slowly and haltingly, but then gain a ste
rhythm that slows a bit toward the end.

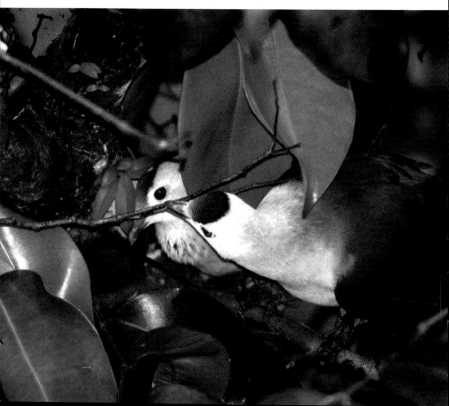

quality of the notes is very much like those of
Palau Owl, and, like the owl, the fruit dove often
s at night. In fact, one can often hear the two
ing together. The notes of the owl have a com-
ely different rhythm and pattern of delivery, and
be differentiated easily once one is familiar with
a calls.

atively little is known about the breeding biology
ne Palau Fruit Dove, but nesting has been re-
ied throughout the year. Courtship behavior has
er been described, but was recently captured in
ographs by MTE. Males and females look much
e, so are distinguished mainly by their behavior,
the female playing a more submissive role. The
e may nibble at the female's face, rather like
ing, and bring her gifts of twigs. The nest, which
rather flimsy platform of twigs in the fork of a
il tree, is often placed in situations that seem
gerously exposed. Both birds participate in
ling the nest, with the male bringing the materi-
and the female having final say as to which
s are used and where they are placed. Some-
s, a lot of bickering is involved. A single white
is incubated by the female, who will abandon
egg and the nest at the slightest disturbance.

Some Palauans claim the female will move the e[gg]
another nest, but such behavior has never been [con]
firmed, and more likely an abandoned egg is q[uickly]
eaten by a predator, and a replacement egg laid [in a]
new nest.

Exactly how long it takes for the egg to hatch [is not]
known. The hatchling is rather ugly compared [to the]
parents, and starts out with black skin sho[wing]
through a thin coat of wispy white down feathers[. The]
flight feathers appear first as pinfeathers with or [blue]
sheaths. Eventually, the chick develops a full c[oat of]
mostly green feathers with a yellow belly. [Each]
feather has a yellow fringe that gradually wears a[way]
so that the birds look very scaly at first but [more]
uniform later. The adult feathers appear in [what]
seems to be a random pattern all over the bod[y so]
that molting birds look rather ragged and bl[otchy.]

Below a chick on the nest, with the first flight fea[thers]
growing in. The top photos on the next page [show]
juvenile fruit doves slowly molting into the specta[cular]
adult colors as shown from the front and back c [in the]
bottom photos. Photos taken on Koror and the [Rock]
Islands.

NICOBAR PIGEON/ LAIB
Caloenas nicobarica pelewensis

C

Columbi

L 35 cm, 14 in. This rather odd-looking large pigeon ranges widely from the namesake Nicobar Island the Indian Ocean to the Solomons in the Pacific, but only on medium to small islands, avoiding the As mainland and bigger islands such as Borneo and New Guinea. This peculiar distribution makes it on the more difficult pigeon species for international birders to observe, and Palau is among the best pla for that. Nicobars nest only on small islands with undisturbed forest, so the Rock Islands are perfect, they visit larger islands to forage. At dawn, flocks of up to 20 pigeons may be seen flying high overh toward the forests of Babeldaob from the Rock Islands and returning late in the day. They are fo throughout the main islands south to Peleliu.

Nicobar Pigeons present a very odd profile, rather like a stealth bomber, because their short white t tend to disappear against a bright sky, and their ruff of long thin feathers around the neck makes the h look tiny. Their wing beats are fast and their flight straight. Other than the tail, the birds are entirely o gray to black, but that does not mean they lack color because their dorsal feathers, especially the l neck hackles, are iridescent with an oil-on-water sheen of blue, green or gold depending on the angl the light. Shimmering in the sun, a Nicobar Pigeon is quite a handsome bird. Adults have a peculiar k over their nostrils, noticeable but not as large as the knob of the Micronesian Imperial Pigeon. Young b in their first year lack the knob on the bill and the neck ruff, and have black tails. Sexes are alike.

Shortly after World War II, the Nicobar Pigeon was reported to be nearly extinct at Palau, but its popula has increased dramatically since then, particularly in recent years since shotguns were banned, but guns are still a problem. Although not abundant, it is not in any immediate danger of extinction.

The Nicobar Pigeon deserves its status as a sp
of conservation concern because the Palau p
tion is an endemic subspecies, the only one
than the nominate, which occupies the rest
species' range. Palau birds are smaller, with s
neck hackles and a less coppery gloss tha
others.

Nicobar Pigeons live in dense forests, where
walk on the ground in search of food, only occa
ally foraging up in the trees. They eat seeds
and sometimes insects or other vertebrates.
can eat much harder nuts than other pigeons c
doves because they have a powerful gizzar
uses ingested rocks to grind up the food. By di
up the food resource in this way, Palau's four
bers of the pigeon family are able to co-exist.

Very little is known about the social behavior of
pigeons, partly because they are rarely observ
the ground. On Peleliu, HDP once observe
birds circling each other and bowing with their
hackles raised. Whether they were courting or
fighting could not be determined. These birds
no vocal sounds whatsoever, nor do they eve
parently. In a family known for its loud and
carrying voices, this species is practically mu
Palau, although it is reported to make a low gr
grunt in other countries.

Nicobar Pigeons nest in trees, often ones that
hang the water in sheltered lagoons. The nes
those of most members of the pigeon family
rather flimsy platform of sticks. Only a single
egg is laid, and it is incubated by both the pa
The hatchling is naked at first and its skin is all
The growth period, during which the chick is f
its parents, is unusually long, reportedly up
months. Once the young bird fledges, it joins it
ents and other adults in the large flocks flying
foraging grounds. Watch for dark-tailed young
among them. The breeding season at Palau
well known, but in other places they breed thr
out the year.

MICRONESIAN IMPERIAL PIGEON/ BELOCHEL
Ducula oceanica

Columb

L 41 cm, 16 in. The Micronesian Imperial Pigeon (formerly just Micronesian Pigeon) is a spectacular
whether seen perched or in flight. The neck, head and chest are pearly gray, the upperparts nearly
with green and coppery reflections, and the underparts are rich orange-chestnut. The bill has a
knob at the base that is thought to grow larger with age. Males have larger and more rounded knobs
the females. In flight, the big pigeon exhibits broad rounded wings and a two-toned profile of gray front,
rear. Flight is straight and direct, with deep wingbeats, and often at great heights.

Micronesian Imperial Pigeons are usually solitary, but sometimes gather in small groups at heavily fr
trees. They eat all kinds of large fleshy fruits and seeds, which they swallow whole. Often, they reveal
presence only by their vocalizations. Their primary call is a spooky-sounding, loud, harsh, booming gro
bark that starts strong and tapers off: *GRAW-raw-aw-aw*. It sounds more like a mammal than a bird.
feeding or sitting quietly, they also frequently utter a deep low moan, similar to some notes of the F
Ground Dove and Palau Fruit Dove, but louder. Imperial pigeons nest high in trees, building a ramsh
pile of sticks. Young birds are less brightly colored than adults, and lack the knob on the bill.

The largest of Palau's pigeons, this bird belongs to a species found on high islands (Yap, Chuuk, Poh
Kosrae) and some atolls across the region east to the Marshall Islands. Although four subspecies
been named, based on slight variations in size and color, their validity is questionable and all look
sound much alike. In Palau, these pigeons are found from Babeldaob to Peleliu, but are rare on the
and anywhere near human habitation. They have traditionally been much pursued by local hunters, an
still considered a delicacy. In earlier times, they were hunted with blowguns and reserved for high
members. Today, people still hunt them with airguns.

SULFUR-CRESTED COCKATOO/ IAKKOTSIANG
Cactua galerita   Psittaci◄

L 50 cm, 20 in. The exact history of how this popular Palauan pet was introduced into the wild is not knc
although folklore abounds. It appeared as a species living in the wild during the 1940s, perhaps origina
from pets liberated by Japanese owners before they were repatriated. The Palauan name is derived ↑
the Japanese. Cockatoos make entertaining and long-lived (up to 60 years) pets, but their loud screec
can be annoying, and they are not good talkers. They are native to Australia and New Guinea, so Pala
not very far from the natural range, and the birds appear to be thriving here. They are most often s
among the Rock Islands from Koror to Mecherchar, and on southern Babeldaob around farms. Sulf
crested Cockatoos raise and lower their yellow crest like a fan, and their fluttery manner of flight is disf
tive. They fly high overhead from island to island, and move about in parties of up to a dozen birds. T
squawks are very similar to those of the Eclectus Parrot, but slightly lower pitched and harsher, with a
syllable *scraw-leek*, the first part harsh, the second a purer tone.

Cockatoos favor big dead trees with large cavities, where they nest between August and January. P
return to the same tree cavity year after year, unless evicted by other cockatoos or Eclectus Parrots. T
lay one or two white eggs, and the hatchlings require up to 2 months to fledge. Young chicks removed f
a nest and handreared make the best pets, but getting up to a nest can be a life-threatening endea
They eat a variety of fruits, seeds and green plant matter, including some favorite human foods. They
agricultural pests on Koror and Babeldaob, raiding fruit crops. But those losses are minor compared to
ecological damage done to the two species of palm endemic to the limestone Rock Island forests (see
account).

ECLECTUS PARROT/ IAKKOTSIANG
Eclectus roratus

Psittaci‹

L 35 cm, 14 in. These colorful parrots were liberated in Palau some time during or just after World Wa
but the exact details are unknown. Like the cockatoos, they are probably descended from Japanese p
and are still popular pets today. In fact, although less friendly, they are much better talkers than cockato
They are unusual among parrots in that the males and females look completely different but equally cc
ful. Males are brilliant green with red sides and wing linings and an orange upper mandible. Females
mostly bright red, with purple-blue upper back, belly and wing linings, a yellow tip to the tail, and an
black bill. Young birds look like their parents as soon as they develop their first coat of feathers. The na
range of the subspecies found in Palau includes New Guinea and associated islands.

In Palau, Eclectus Parrots are found mostly in the Rock Islands from limestone parts of Koror sout
Mecherchar. They are much less numerous than the Sulfur-crested Cockatoos, with whom they may as
ciate, although they are more solitary and rarely seen in flocks. The parrots' loud squawks are simila
those of the cockatoos, but are often paired: *scraw-scrawk!* They have a variety of other odd-soun‹
notes, many with a metallic quality, as in a distinctive *tunk-deee* the first note of which is bell-like,
second more of a whistle.

Eclectus Parrots have strong, direct flight that takes them high over the forest canopy. They like the sa
kinds of huge dead trees for nest cavities as the cockatoos, and have been known to take over cav‹
from the larger birds. They lay one or two eggs between August and January. Eclectus Parrots eat m
the same things as cockatoos (fruits, seeds, leaves, and buds), and unfortunately share their taste for p
hearts. Which of the two species is more damaging to Palau's endemic palm trees (Palau palm *Pty*
sperma, and the Rock Island palm *Gulubia palauensis*) is not known, but both are implicated and are ‹
sidered agricultural pests in Palau. Palms have a single terminal bud from which they grow continually,
this is the "heart of palm" that is also a human delicacy. But eating the heart kills an entire tree, and s‹
parrots love heart of palm, they have nearly wiped out the 2 endemic palm species on Palau.

ORIENTAL CUCKOO/
CHARMUDRENGES
Cuculus saturatus   Cucu

L 33 cm, 13 in. This large cuckoo breeds in ea
Asia and migrates as far as Australia and New Zea
Each year, a few individuals spend their winter in F
They are rather hawk-like in profile, with long po
wings, long tail, and deep swooping flight. In fact
color pattern is not very different from that of so
small accipiters that turn up here. Oriental Cuckoos
two color types or "morphs". Most birds seen are
above and on the breast, with a black-and-white b
belly and a tail with round white spots arranged in
zontal rows. The much less common red or "he
morph (bottom photo) replaces the gray with rust
and is barred all over, with the tail boldly barred ru
black. Both morphs have yellow eyes and bill base
complicate matters, Palau has several confirme
cords for the **Common Cuckoo** *C. canorus*, wh
almost identical in plumage. It differs in having fine
ring on the belly and in voice, which is not he
Palau. However, red morphs of the two specie
easily distinguished by their rump pattern, st
barred in Oriental, plain or with scattered spo
Common. Photos taken on Koror (top) and Ngeru
(bottom) in November.

OTHER CUCKOOS

Four other species of cuckoo (5 if you count one u
firmed sighting of **Asian Koel** *Eudynamis scolopa*
have been recorded at Palau, but all have been
time wonders", birds that showed up only once, anc
never been recorded again. A 19th century naturali
lected the only Palau specimen of **Pacific Long-**
Cuckoo *Urodynamis taitensis*, a bird that breeds i
Zealand and winters among the islands of Polynes
Micronesia but not usually this far west. In Fel
1950, a **Rufous Hawk-Cuckoo** *Hierococcyx*
ythrus was collected on Babeldaob. The species b
in eastern Asia and migrates south to the Philippine
Sulawesi. A **Chestnut-winged Cuckoo** *Clamator*
mandus, a straggler from southeast Asia, was col
on the grounds of what is now the Belau Na
Museum in 1967, and a **Brush Cuckoo** *Cacoman*
riolosus was seen by several ornithologists inc
HDP in June 1978 in the same locality. The latter w
parently a migratory overshoot from Australia. No
these birds were photographed.

Pacific Long-tailed Cuckoo

Brush Cuckoo

Rufous Hawk-Cuckoo

Common Cuckoo

Chestnut-winged Cuckoo

LLARBIRD   V
stomus orientalis   Coraciidae

m, 12 in. The Dollarbird takes its name from a pale spot in its open wing that resembles a silver dollar. ngs to a family called rollers, related to kingfishers, sometimes called the Broad-billed Roller. It is an ooking, big-headed bird whose silhouette can re- e that of a small falcon. It has erratic swooping or g" flight, evident as it hawks for insects on the wing, y darting out and returning to the same exposed . Dollarbirds are most active at dawn or dusk, or cloudy or rainy weather. They are dark blue-green large red bill and a streaked purple patch in the They breed from India and Japan to Australia, but ly rare visitors to Palau. Non-tropical populations igratory, the northern ones flying south in their the Australian ones flying north in theirs, so wan- Dollarbirds could reach Palau in any month of the Most records are of southern birds. They are not re- every year, but in some years several may be nt. Because they perch in the open, they are fairly icuous when they are around. They are usually in the edges of forest, and for some reason seem to perch near taro patches.

Ian Montgomery

PALAU OWL/ CHESUCH
Pyrroglaux podarginus   Strigi

L 23 cm, 9 in. Palau's only owl is not only an endemic species, but an endemic genus. It is the only spe
in its genus, which is therefore called "monotypic" by taxonomists. For a long time, it was thought to be
lated to the scops owl group of Eurasia and Africa, but at present we do not know its true ancestry. It
distinctive and fascinating small owl with mottled brown plumage and big dark brown eyes. Strongly ter
rial, a pair may be found in the same spot day after day. Territories are only about the length of a foo
field in diameter, so up to five individuals can sometimes be heard calling simultaneously. Playing a rec
ing of the bird's call will usually evoke an immediate response to challenge what the owl perceives as a
truder. The bird is certainly common, if not abundant.

Palau Owls roost by day in dense forest, and become active only at dusk. Just before dark, the owl ch
begins, and continues sporadically all night. The individual notes sound somewhat like those of the Pa
Fruit Dove, which also calls at night. But with a little experience, one can distinguish the two easily.
male begins the concert with a monotonous *whock, whock, whock...* that slowly increases in cadence
pitch to reach a climax in about 2 minutes where each note becomes a two-syllabled *whuk-whoo, wl
whoo...* given one per second for half a minute or so. At the climax, the female may also begin to call,
slightly softer notes than the male. Then the male flies toward the female uttering single notes again
drop in volume and pitch to finally fade out completely as he flies to a new perch. Palau Owls call y
round, indicating that they may form permanent pair bonds.

This night hunter finds its prey by sound. It has forward-directed ears, near the eyes, and facial disks
function as parabolic reflectors to concentrate sounds, almost like 3-D hearing...

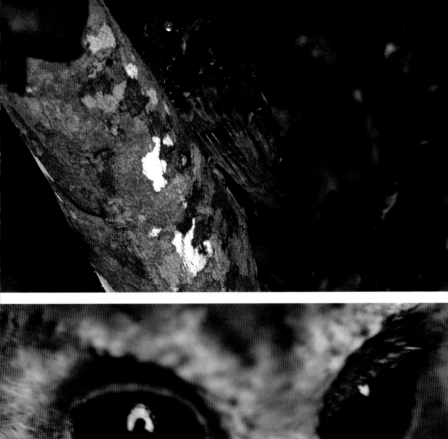

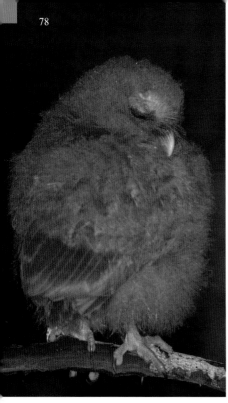

Food is mostly large insects and centipedes, but they also take earthworms and small geckoes.

Their taste for insects got the owls into trouble some years ago, when coconut plantations all over the Pacific were being severely damaged by the introduced Coconut Rhinoceros Beetle *Oryctes rhinoceros*. During the beetle plague, Palau Owls became quite scarce, and were even placed on the U.S. Endangered Species list for a while.

Palau was at the center of the battle to control the beetle, and as the Trust Territory conservation officer at the time told the story to HDP, Palauans were reporting that owls were being killed by beetles that they swallowed whole (and alive!), which then tore their way out of the birds' stomachs! The beetles were said to be able to tear through boards and metal screens also. Someone brought in a dead Palau Owl that had apparently been eviscerated from within. By the late 1960s, these rhinoceros beetles were brought under control by a combination of biological measures developed in Palau, and the owl population has recovered nicely since. Of course, all the evidence is circumstantial, and no direct link was ever proven between rhinoceros beetles and the decline of the owl population, but the story is certainly believable.

Palau Owls breed from April to July. The author last year found a large chick, covered in cream-colored down, but unable to fly with its just-emerging wing feathers, sitting quietly on a bare horizontal branch about 2 m above the ground on Ngeruktabel Island during the day in late April. The adults were nowhere to be seen, but several hours later the chick had disappeared. Presumably, a pair raises only one chick at a time. The nest is a strong, large flat platform of twigs low in a tree.

GRAY NIGHTJAR/ CHEBACHEB
Caprimulgus indicus phalaena

Caprimulg

L 25 cm, 10 in. Also known as the Jungle Nightjar, this is the only nightjar in Micronesia. The endemic P
subspecies belongs to a widespread species found from se. Asia to the Philippines and Indonesia. (
Nightjars live in dense, damp forest where they sleep during the day. The cryptic (camouflage) colora
makes them very hard to find when asleep on a lichen-covered tree branch. They are active from dus
dawn, and in flight, show a narrow white (males) or buff (females) band across the primaries. They are
tributed unevenly from Babeldaob to Peleliu, but are not very common on the Rock Islands. They prefe
forest edge, where they can hawk for insects on the wing, or catch them in aerial sallies from a dead s
A good place to look for them is southern Babeldaob where dense forests border savannas or farml
With a flashlight, one can see the red eye reflections of hunting birds. A captured nightjar brought to I
perched on a railing of her patio and dashed out after large moths attracted by the lights, ignoring ne
geckos, before flying off. Most local people have never seen this bird, but Palauans know its pec
knocking voice. Legend has it that a nightjar calling near a dwelling means someone there is pregnant!
"song" is a series of sharp low-pitched notes like the sound of a small hammer on hard wood. These gr
ally increase in speed and pitch *tawk tock tac-tac-tac-tac*. Sometimes several birds may call together in
santly for several minutes. Flying birds utter other sounds such as a rasping snore and a screechy *kre
kreek*. Like the Palau Owl, Gray Nightjars respond to playback of their song. In this way, HDP once ent
a bird to fly out of the forest and land at his feet!

Nothing is known about the nesting behavior in Palau. Elsewhere, nightjars lay their eggs in a slight sc
on open level ground under a tree, with 1-2 eggs. Like the Palau Owl, the Gray Nightjars are very territo
and a pair will stay around the same area year round.

Michelle & Peter Wong

PALAU SWIFTLET/ CHESISEKIAID
Aerodramus pelewensis

Apodid

L 10 cm, 4 in. Palau Swiftlets, though not colorful, are wonderful to watch as they fly acrobatica
over forest and town. The genus name in Latin means "air runner" and it is an appropriate designatie
In fact, swiftlets are unable to perch on branches of trees, but are only able to cling with their tiny feet
vertical surfaces such as the walls of caves where they nest. Away from the cave, they are in consta
flight. They can be seen almost any time of day from Babeldaob to Peleliu. Palau Swiftlets were on
considered the same species as other swiftlets in Micronesia, but differences in such things as how t
nests are constructed now indicate that there are several species involved. The Palau one is somewl
darker and glossier on the back than the others, and has a pale patch on the rump. The pale rump
quite variable, and some individuals show very little, although most clearly have it. The patch is oft
mottled with gray-brown and is never sharply defined with clean margins as in some larger swifts t
could be seen in Palau.

Another difference is the distinctive insect-like, squeaky or chattering vocalization uttered while one b
is chasing another. This call is only rarely heard, and may be associated with courtship. Other swiftle
in Micronesia are completely silent until they enter a cave. Whether the Palau Swiftlet uses echolocati
to navigate in the darkness is not known. Related species in the Caroline Islands do, and when th
enter a cave, they make a steady clicking sound, the echoes of which tell the birds where the walls a
so they do not crash. It is a bit like radar. Palau Swiftlets usually do not nest so deep inside a cave t
this ability would be necessary, but many deep potential caves have not been explored. As with ma
Palau birds, much remains to be learned.

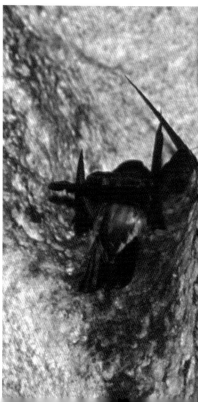

Palau Swiftlets make their nests almost entirely mosses, plucked on the wing from trees. These wreathed together and glued to the cave wall v a special heavy saliva. Related species in sot east Asia make their nests entirely of saliva, wh hardens into a rubbery cup. These are harves and used as the base for bird's nest soup, cons ered a special delicacy. Luckily for the Palau t its nest is not usable for human food. The nests often in clusters of dozens or more, and space r be shared with sheathtail bats. In the cup of mc the mother swiftlet lays her single nearly spher white egg. The chick has pink skin at first, but t develops a coat of dark feathers.

The swiftlets' whole diet consists of flying inse which they catch on the wing. When feec young, a bird will build up a huge mass, calle bolus, of flies, mosquitoes, and other inse before returning to feed the chick. One can son times see their bulging throats as they fly p. Imagine how many more annoying insects wc be around without the natural control of swift and bats...

Although the nest caves are relatively safe fi

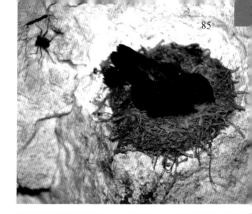

emies, there are dangers. Sometimes light-
ot crabs *Grapsus sp.* are able to catch incu-
ting birds or chicks, but more often they scav-
ge the carcasses of birds that die and fall to
e cave floors.

the course of photographing the nest cycle,
TE discovered an interesting relationship that
not yet understood by science. A common
ve inhabitant in Palau is a large arthropod
lled an amblypigid. It looks like something
m a horror movie, and is more closely related
spiders and scorpions than to insects. Am-
pigids usually eat cave crickets, but here are
und in caves where only swiftlets and bats
e, and almost every swiftlet nest with a chick
ems to have a young amblypigid in atten-
nce. Just what it is doing there is a mystery,
t maybe it picks up food items dropped by the
ds. The swiftlets ignore them, and the young
nblypigids are not big enough yet to be a
eat to the birds. The biggest threat to nesting
viftlets is human disturbance. When people
ter a nest cave, the birds panic and fly
und, possibly dislodging eggs and leaving
cks unattended.

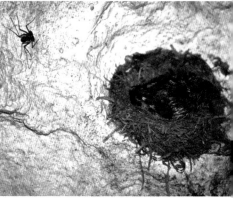

RUSTY- CAPPED KINGFISHER/
CHEROSECH, ONGELIMADECH
Todiramphus cinnamominus pelewensis   Alcedinid

L 20 cm, 8 in. In most previous books this bird has been called Micronesian Kingfisher because it was garded as one of 3 subspecies that make up that species. However, HDP has accumulated eviden (see below) that shows that those 3 supposed subspecies could not possibly interbreed successf and that there is really no such thing as the "Micronesian Kingfisher". Until the details are properly p lished, however, we continue to use the traditional taxonomy, but re-christen this endemic Palau soo to-be species with a distinctive English name. It is found from Babeldaob to Peleliu.

This is the smaller of Palau's 2 kingfishers, and a much less familiar and less conspicuous bird than boisterous cousin, the Collared Kingfisher. It has a similar color pattern, with dark greenish blue ba wings, and tail and white collar and underparts, but the crown is pale with a variable tinge of rusty-orar (birds with very worn feathers look almost white-capped). It has a very distinctive upright posture. Ma and females are identical in color, and young birds look just like the adults except that the side bre feathers have thin dark fringes at their tips.

The Rusty-capped Kingfisher is a retiring denizen of dense forests that sits motionless for long peric in shady vegetation near the forest floor. Joe Marshall, an ornithologist who visited Palau shortly af World War II, claimed that this bird would fly only when one attempted to grab it. He probably encot tered a juvenile bird, since the parents often "park" young chicks for long periods while they go off a hunt. Sometimes they perch out in the open, also on powerlines along the Compact Road on Babeldac They are territorial year round, and members of a pair can be found in the same area day after day.

Unlike the highly vocal Collared Kingfis
Rusty-caps are usually silent, and only c
dawn and dusk, or when they call their c
When they do call, their voice is harshe
otherwise rather similar to some calls of the
lared Kingfisher. They more often utter
slower call, beginning with several his
screeches, followed by a series of drawn
quavering notes: scheee-scheee-scheee-k
e-ek, kree-e-ek, kree-e-ek. Birders find it di
to tell the two species apart on voice alone

These birds are wait-and-pounce hur
catching lizards and large insects, but the
tails of their diet are not well known.
watching a nesting pair near her house,
made the interesting discovery that, like r
kingfishers, this one coughs up pellets (m
photo) that contain the indigestible hard pa
their prey. They do so in the same place e
day, and future studies of these pellets
reveal exactly what these birds eat.

The nest of this kingfisher is built in a cavity
in a tree, which a pair may use year after
Nesting begins in late summer, and the s
chick begins to fly by September, but the e
incubation and nestling periods are not kn
The chick remains with its parents for up
year, and often roosts with the female.

Differences among the so-called "Micron
Kingfishers" include voice, adult and juv
plumage coloration, and nesting habits. T
on Pohnpei are larger, and look very mucl
Rusty-caps as adults, but the juveniles
semble the strikingly different Guam kingf
In that one, the white parts of the Rusty-
plumage are a rich rusty chestnut, and, u
the other 2, adult females are distinctive v
white belly, but juveniles are like adults. T
visual differences are what scientists ca
"isolating mechanism". This is any behav
ecological or physical chracteristic that pre
two species from interbreeding, during
mating process or after pairs have formed
example, Pohnpei kingfishers nest in cavit
termite nests, while the Rusty-capped uses
cavities, since the termite nests in Pala
used by Collared Kingfishers. So even if,
thetically, a Pohnpei bird and Rusty-cap v
mate, they would not be able to decide whe
nest! And we suspect that the 3 Micron
forms might not recognize each other vis
either.

COLLARED KINGFISHER/ TENGADIDIK
Todiramphus chloris teraokai   Alcedinic

L 24 cm, 9.5 in. Kingfishers are so named because many species feed mainly by diving into the wa
to catch fish. One group, however, called forest kingfishers, do not dive and more often feed away fr
water. Both of Palau's kingfishers are forest kingfishers, although this larger species can also be se
along shorelines. The Collared Kingfisher is distributed throughout Palau, including all the Southwest
lands, and can be found in all habitats, although it tends to leave the dense forest interior more to
Rusty-capped Kingfisher. It can commonly be seen feeding along the shore or on exposed flats at
tide, or perching on an exposed snag or on powerlines along the road. It is boldly patterned with iridesc
blue crown, wings and tail, white collar and underparts. Usually a white spot is conspicuous in the lo
and may extend back as a broken white eyebrow. Broad black eyestripes encircle and meet on the na
and there is no hint of rust color in the plumage. Young birds look like brown or green-tinged adults v
some fine barring, sometimes slightly tinged with rust, at the sides of the breast.

The Collared Kingfisher eats virtually anything it can catch, including small fish, lizards, insects, spide
crabs, and mice. It beats its prey to death against a tree branch or by pecking at the head, then swallo
it whole. Sometimes the tail of a gecko or mouse will trail outside the bird's mouth for several minute:
also kills small birds, including chicks of domestic chickens, by dive-bombing and spearing them in
head. Sometimes, they also take eggs from nests. At Palau, this kingfisher fills the ecological role o
small raptor, even though it is not one. As with raptors elsewhere, a lone kingfisher may be mobbed
small birds, especially white-eyes, who gather around it and chatter loudly until the predator flies off.
other feeding method involves hovering and picking large insects or other prey from the outer branc
of trees. Palauan chicken farmers consider this bird a pest, and it is one of only two native birds not p
tected by law. They are quite wary and usually fly immediately when approached too closely.

As they fly away, they give loud alarm calls *peep, chup-eep*... or an incisive *keep-keep-kee*, the calls can run together. They may also give latter call from a perch, accompanied by an up flip of the tail. When sitting quietly, Collared K fishers may utter a slow, drawn out *chupweeee* last note quavering slightly. They are much no than the Rusty-capped Kingfishers.

Collared Kingfishers at Palau are usually four pairs, defending a territory. The nesting season July and August. They sometimes nest in na tree cavities, but more often they hollow out a in a termite nest as seen here. Usually 2 unma white eggs are laid. Hatchlings are naked, with skin, but soon develop pin feathers with a color tern mimicking that of the adult. Both parents the chicks on crabs, lizards, insects and small Kingfishers are not very tidy housekeepers, droppings of the chicks accumulate in the nest it is quite smelly. By the time the chicks fle about 4 weeks after hatching, their plumage ma heavily matted with excrement.

The Collared Kingfisher of Palau is the local re sentative of a species that ranges from the Red to Samoa, and has more named subspecies than any other bird. Almost certainly, some of th subspecies are actually full species, but the P one is probably not one of them because the d ences that make it endemic subspecies seem tively minor. But ongoing studies of vocalizati nesting habits, and genetics (DNA) could reveal it is just as distinctive in the kingfisher context as Rusty-capped Kingfisher is.

MICRONESIAN MYZOMELA/ CHESISEBANGIAU
Myzomela rubratra kobayashii   Meliphagidi

L 13 cm, 5 in. This vivid little red and black bird is one of the most familiar in Palau. Formerly called the cronesian Honeyeater, it and other members of its genus now use the genus name Myzom (pronounced *MY-zo-MELL-a*, NOT *my-ZOM-el-a*) which roughly means "eats honey", as the English na to distinguish this group of small birds from the larger members of their family. In Palau, the distinctio not important because the Micronesian Myzomela is the only honeyeater present. They are found or the larger islands of Micronesia, but each island population has enough distinctive features to be rec nized as a subspecies. Closely related birds, formerly considered the same species, are also foun Melanesia and Samoa, and all of them together make up what is known as the Cardinal Myzomela c plex.

Honeyeaters are so named because they feed mostly on the nectar of flowers. This habit often brings cronesian Myzomelas into yards, parks, and hotel grounds where there are flowers in bloom. Like all h eyeaters, they have a special adapted tongue divided into 4 parts at the tip, and then subdivided in fringe that makes it look like a tiny brush or mop. And the birds do, indeed, mop up the "honey" from t favorite flowers (birds cannot suck; they depend on capillary action to sip liquids). They are very ac feeders, moving from flower to flower quickly, and spending as little as 2 seconds at each. Despite t small size, Micronesian Myzomelas are very aggressive, and chase other larger birds away from their vorite flowering trees. Pairs often set up a regular circuit that they patrol on a cycle that allows the flow to replenish their nectar between visits. To ecologists, this kind of feeding is known as "trap-lining", ar is found in a wide variety of unrelated nectar-feeding birds. To supplement their largely carbohydrate c myzomelas also eat insects and snails.

97

Juv

The brilliant crimson and black males of the M
nesian Myzomela are rather similar from islar
island, differing mainly in subtle shades of
(Palau birds are more crimson, those in the N
anas more orange, etc.), but the females vary
ticeably. Palau females are relatively bright,
almost as much red as the male but no black, w
is replaced by olive brown. Juveniles can be di
guished by their yellow rictus (corner of the mc
but otherwise resemble adults except that the v
feathers are brownish gray rather than black,
narrow olive-yellow or red edging. There is a f
wide variation within island populations as we
between them.

These birds nest throughout the year. The nest
lightly constructed cup woven from grasses and
stems, with some strands of green moss on the
side. It is usually suspended in a horizontal fork
small tree about 2m from the ground, but the k
are versatile and may even build their nest
potted plants near houses. The two, or rarely t
eggs are white, with reddish brown spots on th

ger end and are incubated only by the female.
[ma]les help with feeding nestlings and with carry-
[ing] droppings away from the nest. Because they
[ne]ed the protein for growth, the chicks' diet is
[mo]stly insects rather than nectar. At hatching,
[the] young have only a few wisps of gray down,
[bu]t soon develop a full coat. The nestlings' bills
[are] bright yellow inside and out, rather than
[bla]ck as in the adults. The chicks fledge in about
[two] weeks, but continue to be fed by their parents
[for] some time after that. The male vigorously de-
[fen]ds the nest, chasing away much larger birds,
[esp]ecially known nest robbers such as kingfish-
[er]s and starlings. If an intruder gets very close to
[the] chicks, the female will pretend to be hurt, flut-
[ter]ing on the ground and using only one wing.
[Su]ch distraction behavior serves to lure the in-
[tru]der away from the nest.

[Mi]cronesian Myzomelas are found throughout
[Pal]au except for the Southwest Islands. They
[are] seen in all terrestrial habitats, including coco-
[nut] groves and mangroves, but are less

common in dense forest. They usually feed in canopy or in flowering shrubs rather than in understory, and are often seen flying high o the trees, especially when engaged in fights rivals. Fights can get so heated, that the two r birds will fall to the ground and forget everyth around them. Because many island flowers dep on birds for pollination, myzomelas perform an portant function in the environment.

The most commonly heard sounds from these b are buzzy chirps, whistles, and raspy scol notes. None of the daytime vocalizations repre the territorial song, however. That is reserved pre-dawn hours when it is still dark. Then, m sing a long and complex whistled melody, us from the same perch day after day. Often, man dividuals may be heard from one spot formir single-species dawn chorus. The chorus contir vigorously until there is just enough light to see then, almost as if someone suddenly pulled plug, every bird stops singing at the same time, the song is not heard again until the next morr The various myzomela subspecies differ somev in their dawn songs, but we do not yet know the nificance of the variation.

PALAU WOODSWALLOW/ MENGALULIU
Artamus leucorhynchus pelewensis   Artamid.

L 18 cm, 7 in. The Palau Woodswallow is a handsome bird that looks as if it is dressed up in a tuxe
The head and upper breast, wings, upper back, and tail are sooty black, while the underparts and rur
are pure white. The bill is pale blue with a black tip. Juveniles differ in having pale buffy white edgings
their dorsal feathers that make them look scaly, a yellowish pink bill, and a blurry boundary between t
black throat and the white breast. They are conspicuous birds that perch in the open or fly about, hawki
insects in the air. Their flight is graceful and acrobatic, alternating quick flapping with gliding on fix
wings. They also feed by aerial sallies, flying out from a perch, snagging an insect, and returning to t
same spot. They are not shy, and can often be approached closely. If you stay in their area long enoug
they may actually fly over and check you out. They are highly social, usually in small groups of 2-5 bir
that may crowd together on a perch, with no space between individuals. At night, up to ten birds m
gather together to roost.

Woodswallows are attracted to areas that have been burned, perhaps because such places have ma
dead snags for perches and nest sites. The breeding habits of Palau Woodswallows are not well know
A nest discovered in June 1978 by Peace Corps ornithologist John Engbring, was a bowl woven of fi
grasses on a horizontal branch of a large tree at the edge of a savannah. It held two nearly grown flec
lings. MTE has photographed adults with older juvenile birds in previous years around May (see n
pages), and observed parents flying back and forth to a nest with food in May of 2007. The nest was h
up in a tree, too high to get to or be able to photograph it. It was in a dense forest area, also at the ed
of a savannah, and the parent birds would swoop down and dive-bomb her when she came close to t
nest tree. So the breeding season is probably from about March to July.

The Palau Woodswallow's call is a loud *kewick*
the song, as described by Engbring, includes "a v
ety of soft, mellow buzzing, warbling, and chuck
notes."

The Palau Woodswallow is also one of Palau's ra
endemic birds, with only a few hundred of th
inhabiting the open savannahs of northern Ba
daob. Because of its friendliness and limited hab
it is no match for boys with airguns, and needs urg
protection for it to be able to survive on Babeldac
the coming years.

A few individuals occasionally visit Koror and
Rock Islands. The Palau bird is a subspecies of
White-breasted Woodswallow that ranges from
laysia to Australia, but differs from all but one o
subspecies in being nearly black rather than g
and possibly in vocalizations. Whether these di
ences are sufficient to consider it a full species is
rently under investigation by HDP.

PALAU CICADABIRD/ KIUIDUKALL

Coracina tenuirostris monacha   **e**

Campephagidae

L 18 cm, 7 in. The Palau Cicadabird belongs to a family of the Australasian region known as cuck[e] shrikes because they have characteristics of both true cuckoos and true shrikes, but are neither. It is quiet, inconspicuous, and rather mysterious bird, widespread in forests from Babeldaob to Peleliu, but common anywhere. The male is bluish slate all over, with black lores and pale edgings to the wing fea ers. The female is very different, brownish gray above, honey-colored below, with black chevron-shap spots on the sides of the breast and bars on the flanks. A black eyestripe and pale eyebrow give he facial expression unlike that of any other Palau bird except perhaps the Palau Bush Warbler. She a has fairly broad honey-colored edging on the wing feathers. Juveniles of both sexes look like the fem but may have more pale feather edges above.

Cicadabirds may be found as singles, pairs, or small family groups. Their movements are slow and de erate, making them hard to locate in dense foliage. As they forage, they have a characteristic swivel movement of the head (see below) as they peer underneath leaves. It is this movement, along with barred plumage of the female, that reminded Europeans of cuckoos. It was the bill, with a slight hook the tip, that reminded them of shrikes. Their food includes insects, usually plucked from branches leaves, and sometimes snatched from mid-air, and small berry-like fruits. They usually keep to the for canopy, but at the forest edge, such as the borders of savannahs on Babeldaob, or where trees overha the water in the Rock Islands, they may come down to eye level.

The name cicadabird comes from the fact that similar birds in Australia have loud vocalizations like sound of cicadas. Currently, those birds and the Palau Cicadabird are considered the same species, that is about to change. For one thing, the Palau bird sounds nothing at all like a cicada.

In fact, the Palau bird sounds like nothing at most of the time! It is one of the quietest birds the Palau forest. The most frequently heard ca an inconspicuous upslurred whistle: *tuweep*. I the way members of a pair keep track of ea other as they move slowly through the trees. T whistle also forms part of the bird's song, whicł very rarely heard and was only recently record by HDP near Lake Ngardok. John Engbring, w spent years working with Palauan birds, nev heard the song. In addition to both upslurred a downslurred whistles, the song includes ha raspy notes given in groups of 3, and other chir and warbles.

The breeding habits of the Palau Cicadabird completely unknown. No nest has ever been ported, so the first one to be found will be an portant discovery. Outside Palau, cicadabi build shallow cup nests of twigs bound with spi webs and camouflaged with lichens on a high h zontal branch of a large tree. For some reas female cicadabirds are more readily seen at Pa than males. From a distance, especially with good light, the male is easily mistaken for Morningbird or Starling.

The widespread species to which the Palau Ci dabird supposedly belongs ranges from north Australia to eastern Indonesia, New Guinea, Solomon Islands, and Micronesia. The numerc subspecies differ greatly among themselves female plumage, size, and vocalizations and ma of them are good candidates for full spec status. Two other "subspecies" are found in Mic nesia. The one on Yap resembles the Palau Cic abird, but the female is a much darker reddis brown color, and the Yap bird is so much lar that it probably could not succesfully mate wit Palau bird. On Pohnpei, there is a cicadabird t has very different female colors (gray and chest with no bars) and a completely different so which, again, sounds nothing like a cicada! Al these birds are poorly known, and just as unco mon and mysterious as the Palau Cicadabird.

Good areas to look for cicadabirds in Palau are entrance to the Lake Ngardok trail, the Koror R ervoir in Airai, and the old lighthouse trail Ngeruktabel.

MORNINGBIRD/ TUTAU
Colluricincla tenebrosa

Colluricinclid

L 19 cm, 7.5 in. The Morningbird is known to everyone in Palau by its beautiful melodic song that is of the first sound in the dawn chorus. The song includes liquid chirps and whistles, often grouped into sh bursts, that usually start high and end low, but otherwise seem almost random. After the dawn chor Morningbirds are mostly silent except during the first part of the year when they are nesting and defend territories. When disturbed or irritated, they utter a harsh series of drawn-out raspy notes.

Considering their beautiful songs, Morningbirds are disappointingly drab in appearance. Adults are all d sooty gray, with no prominent markings or bright colors. They could be confused with the Micronesian St ling, but are not glossy and lack the bright yellow eyes of that bird, or with the male Palau Cicadabird, wh is a smoother, bluer gray. Younger birds tend to be a paler rusty brown, with only the head and chest so gray, giving them a hooded look. They belong to a family of the Australasian region known as shrik thrushes, because they are thrushlike in behavior but have heavy hooked bills like those of shrikes.

Morningbirds are fairly common in deep forests from Babeldaob to Peleliu, where they feed near ground or at mid-level, rarely in the canopy. Although they are skulkers in the shadows, they are easy see because they are so curious, especially young birds. They often approach humans closely, and ev follow them through the forest, peering inquisitively at the intruders. They frequently hold the bill sligl open as if about to ask a question. They are omnivores that pick fruits and berries as well as insects a other small invertebrates from the trunks and branches of trees. Morningbirds are usually solitary, but n sometimes gather in loose groups of 4 or 5 birds. They are often seen near the ground picking fights v the Palau Fantail over food. The nest of the Morningbird has never been discovered, so its breeding b logy is completely unknown. MTE has seen begging juveniles being fed in April, May, and October.

PALAU FANTAIL/ MELIMDELEBTEB, CHESISIRECH
Rhipidura lepida

Rhipidurida

L 15 cm, 6 in. One of Palau's most beautiful and appealing endemics, the Palau Fantail lives in all kin
of forest, but it is especially fond of open, second-growth habitats and ravine forests. Consequently
can be seen close to towns and villages from Babeldaob to Peleliu. It has two Palauan names, t
second one used only on Peleliu. It is a striking bird both because of its bold colors and its unique beha
ior. Adults are bright rusty red, close to what artists call "Chinese orange", on the upperparts and the re
underparts. The rest of the underside is white, divided by a bold black band separating the throat fro
the breast. The lores and auricular patch are dark brown. The primaries and tail feathers are dus
brown, the latter boldly tipped with rusty red, forming a band at the tip of the tail. The fantail is so nam
because it often fans its tail broadly when excited. It also often folds the tail and wags it back and for
A further postural peculiarity is that the wings are held loosely, often drooping at the sides. Males and
males look just alike, but can be distinguished by their different behavior at the nest (see belov

Palau Fantails are almost entirely insectivorous, picking their prey from leaves of trees or snatching the
from midair. They are very active foragers from the ground to the highest canopy and may even enga
in piracy. MTE has seen them attack and steal food items from Morningbirds, Giant White-eyes, a
even from a Palau Ground Dove. They often follow other birds around when they are foraging, waiti
for their chance. While feeding, they utter characteristic squeaky, downslurred *keee-er* call notes th
may be in series of 3: *KEE-keer-kew!* The song is much less often heard, and is more likely to be giv
in the morning. It is a rapid jumble of high squeaky notes.

The breeding biology of the Palau Fantail is comparatively well known, and nesting occurs throughc
the year. It begins with a mating display in which the male lifts and fans his tail broadly as he parad
before the female. Fantail pairs are highly territorial, and both male and female will defend the ne
dive-bombing and fluttering around intruders, wings drooped and fanned tail held high, making a lot
noise. Nests are often built near a rock ledge, and often near or in a **rebotel** wax apple tree *Eugenia*
vanica.

The nest is a dainty, tightly woven cup of p[...]
fibers and bark strips situated in a fork like a cup[...]
a saucer. Below the nest is a "tail" several centi[...]
ters long that gives the whole nest the look of an[...]
cream cone. Fantails often recycle old ne[...]
either reusing the nest as it is or using the mater[...]
in a new one.

The single egg is white, speckled all over [...]
reddish-brown, and is incubated only by the [...]
male. The male approaches every 20 minutes[...]
so, and the two fly off together to forage for a [...]
minutes, but only the female returns to the e[...]
The incubation time is not known exactly, bu[...]
around 2-3 weeks. The tiny hatchling is naked [...]
pink, but soon develops some sparse chestn[...]
colored down. It is fed by both parents, tiny inse[...]
at first, then larger items such as moths and cr[...]
ets. When approaching the nest to feed, the fem[...]
always takes the same stealthy, round-about [...]
proach, but the male flies directly to the nest, fe[...]
fast, and returns to his job as sentinel. Fledgl[...]
are rusty-brown, and lack the bold breast patter[...]
the adults. They may continue to be fed by t[...]
parents for several weeks.

rprisingly, Palau Fantail nests are often out in
e open, with little or no concealment, and the
ds spend a lot of their energy defending them
ainst predators. Larger birds that pose little
eat, such as megapodes, are tolerated nearby,
t kingfishers, starlings, and Morningbirds, as
Il as geckoes and skinks are attacked by both
ale and female if they come within 30 feet of the
st. That is with good reason, because MTE
s observed a Collared Kingfisher flying away
th a fantail egg in its bill.

her predators may include one or both of the
ɔ species of small Palau forest snakes, the
w Palau Boa *Candoia superciliosa*, or the fast
lau Racer *Dendrelaphis sp.* MTE recently pho-
graphed a pair of nesting fantails hysterically
acking a small boa near their nest, which had
atchling in it. The snake showed no interest in
e nest or hatchling at all, but both birds kept
cking at the snake's body, always avoiding the
ad, until the hapless reptile dropped to the
ound and moved away from the area. Perhaps
snakes only take the eggs, or the birds had
wrong species of snake.

Out of 13 Palau Fantail nests observed by M[...] only 2 successfully fledged a chick. The oth[...] were lost to predators or storms. Two in thirt[...] may seem like rather long odds for survival of[...] species, but in fact, such low success is typica[...] tropical birds worldwide. Only a small percent[...] of nests actually produce the next generation,[...] once a bird fledges, it stands a good chance of l[...] term survival, and one pair may have many [...] spring over a period of years. In any case, [...] Palau Fantail is doing well, having recovered fr[...] a period around World War II when it had beco[...] rather scarce. Interestingly, it was nearly wiped [...] on Peleliu at that time, where it is abundant tod[...]

Many Palauans know how to imitate the call of [...] Fantail, and if it sounds close enough, the bird [...] often come down to eye level and scold the [...] truder loudly. Young birds that still lack the w[...] underside are often very curious and can easily [...] approached closely. The parents are usually cl[...] by, and will swoop down to guide the young [...] away from danger. Begging juvenile birds [...] "parked" on a branch by the parents, where t[...] call out loudly, spreading their wings and flutte[...] them around when they want to get fed.

PALAU FLYCATCHER/ CHARMELACHULL
Myiagra erythrops

Monarchi◼

L 13 cm, 5 in. The charming and inquisitive Palau Flycatcher is one of the islands' most familiar ende◼
ics. It inhabits all types of forest from Babeldaob to Peleliu, and is particularly common in mangro◼
(which is why it has been called Mangrove Flycatcher in some books). It belongs to a genus of small
sectivorous birds that are widespread on islands of the tropical Pacific, including other high islar◼
(Guam, where now extinct; Chuuk; and Pohnpei) in Micronesia. All *Myiagra* flycatchers have whist
songs and raspy call notes, and catch insects on the wing. The four in Micronesia were once conside◼
subspecies of a single species, which may be listed under the obsolete names Micronesian Flycatc◼
or Micronesian Broadbill in older literature, but their obvious differences in plumage color, voice and s◼
reveal them to be separate species.

The Palau Flycatcher is a handsome little bird, with a slaty-blue top, side and underparts that are wh◼
at the rear and salmon-red at the front. The salmon color encircles the eye and it is the source of the La◼
name *erythrops* (=red-eye) although the eye itself is dark brown. Males are more richly colored than ◼
males, but the patterns are very similar. Females are browner above, and the intensity of the salmon-◼
color on the face and breast varies individually. From the side, the bill looks thin, but from above or bel◼
it is very wide, almost triangular. The broad bill, along with prominent "whiskers" called rectal bristle◼
the sides, forms an excellent trap for snatching flying insects out of the air. One can easily hear the s◼
prisingly loud bill snap.

Palau Flycatchers are conspicious not only because of their feeding habits, but also because they are◼
feisty. They often fly across trails or perch in the open where they are easy to observe.

♂

♀

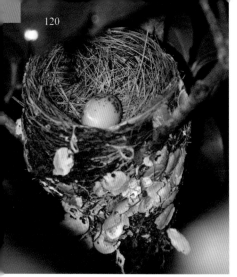

The Flycatchers regularly approach people w
in the forest and scold the intruders with short,
notes: *zhrick, zhrick, zhrick,* etc. The territoria
is very different, a pleasing and energetic ser
4-5 pure whistles all on the same note, or a
series of 7-8 whistles that drop in pitch. The
most often in the morning.

Flycatchers breed between October and May
perhaps also other months. The nest is one
most beautifully crafted of any in Palau. It is a
woven bowl of plant fibers, grasses, and stem
is decorated on the outside with round white
that resemble lichens, but are actually inside-o
cases of spiders! The nest is usually situatec
fork of a tree fairly high off the ground, and co
only one egg. It is vigorously defended by bot
ents, who utter a distinctive call to warn each
whenever a predator gets too close. Nest-raide
clude boas, large skinks, and monitor lizards a
as other birds such as kingfishers and starlings
flycatchers fly around the predators and fear
dive-bomb them with their bills to drive them
but Micronesian Starlings are known to gang u
steal eggs by force of numbers. Of 8 nests s
recently by MTE, five lost their eggs before
could hatch, three hatched, but only two of
survived to fledging. This again demonstrate
long odds of any given egg being successfull
tropics.

The egg, which is white with a circle of red
brown spots on the larger end, is incubated by
male and female alternately, and both feed the
Incubation takes about a month, and the
spends another month in the nest before fledg
is fed increasingly larger insects as it grows
chick's droppings are produced in a small me
nous sack that is immediately carried away
parents. The fledgling (top right) wears a plu
that was apparently never described before MT
this photo in 2007. It is much less colorful tha
adults, lacks the broad pale area on the fore
and has a dark patch in the auriculars. It also s
broad buffy-white edgings to the wing feathers
white tip to the tail. Older birds (middle right)
their first year have a plumage that resembles
the adult but paler.

Michelle & Peter Wong

BARN SWALLOW/ TSUBAME
Hirundo rustica   Hirundir

L 18 cm, 7 in. The Barn Swallow is a widesprea
common bird throughout the northern hemisı
and a nonbreeding visitor to Palau, mainly durir
winter months but with a few individuals are pr
most of the year. The local name is actual
Japanese word for "swallow". Barn swallow
easily recognized by their long, deeply forked
but most of those seen in Palau are immature
shorter tail feathers. Both adults and younger
are dark above and white below. First-year
have pale foreheads, but by spring, many hav
chestnut forehead and throat and dark breast
of the adult plumage. Adults are glossy blue-
above with some white spots near the base
tail. Barn Swallows are usually seen in small to
flocks. They often hang around buildings (su
barns, where they often nest) and are familiar
in Palauan villages, where they may perch in
on power lines. They are graceful and acroba
flight, catching their insect food on the wing.
long tail streamers apparently help them mar
in the air in pursuit of prey. Probably because
tracts large numbers of flies and other insect
Koror landfill is Barn Swallow headquarters in
and hundreds may gather there. Barn Swallow
be quite vocal, usually giving their twittering ca
the wing. They sometimes ingest small stones
the ground. Another swallow, the **Asian**
Martin *Delichon dasypus* is a rare visitor to Pa
is clean black above and white below, with a
nent white rump and no breast band.

GRAY-STREAKED
FLYCATCHER
Muscicapa   greseisticta   Muscica

L 15 cm, 6 in. This drab brownish gray bir
eastern Asia is a rare visitor to Palau durir
northern winter. Although not numerous, at I
few individuals seem to be present each yea
they are noticeable because they often sit on
exposed perches. From these vantage points
dart out and snatch flying insects, then usually
to the same perch. They are stocky, shor
birds, and the only species regularly seen at
that is prominently streaked below.

RASIAN TREE SPARROW **A**
r montanus   Passeridae

m, 5.5 in. This bird is Palau's newest avian im-
t. A few were discovered on Peleliu in 2000,
nce then that population has increased to sev-
ozen, mostly in the village of Kloulklubed. By
a small population (under 30) had become es-
ed around the harbor area of Malakal, and
ow spread to other urban areas around Koror.
er these birds were purposely brought in or
iked a ride on cargo ships is not known. They
ative to Japan and the Philippines, introduced
ell-established in the Marianas and Guam, and
ive close to ports. All authors who have re-
on the Eurasian Tree Sparrow at Palau have
ated that they be exterminated before the
tions become too large, but so far nothing has
one to control them. Whether they are a seri-
reat to native birds is debatable, but history
own that the introduction of alien species to is-
s never a good idea. These sparrows feed on
and scraps of garbage. They are gregarious
ten sit on power lines and fences. They build
ests in the eaves of buildings or other man-
structures, and lay 2-5 speckled eggs.

PALAU BUSH WARBLER/ WUUL or CHESISEBARSECH

Cettia annae   Sylvii

L 15 cm, 6 in. This fascinating Palau endemic could well be called the Voice of Palau. Its eerie, melanc whistles color the island forest soundscape for much of the year. The typical song begins with a l pitched flute-like note *wooooooOOOOO* that swells in volume and may be sustained for as long as a second. One bird may answer another, picking up the whistle at a slightly different pitch as the first starts to fade. Then a third may chime in, and so it goes so that the listener might think it was a single whistle that changed pitch, except for the fact that the tones often overlap to produce mournful harmo or close dissonances. Sometimes the singer stutters a bit at the start of the whistle: *oo-oo-ooOOOOOO*. The effect is somewhat like that of an orchestral string section tuning up. Sometimes whistle, which is probably imitated by the bird's Palauan name, is the whole song, but often a rapid ju of chirps and warbles, or a few quick whistles at different pitches, marks the end of a single utteranc "strophe". The Palau Bush Warbler also sings a second, totally different song of chirps and warbles sounds a lot like that of the Micronesian Myzomela, and like it is most often sung at dawn. Singing is sonal, and bush warblers go silent when they are not breeding, usually during the months of the nort winter, but there is some variation year to year, probably related to weather. Peak singing is in June July, when the bush warbler's whistles often provide a continuous background for other bird songs.

Palau Bush Warblers sing from concealment in the forest underbrush, often within a meter or 2 of ground. They seem to love hiding in dense vine tangles, where they are nearly impossible to see des their enticing song. Birds can sometimes be lured into view by an imitation of their whistles, which are within human range. When disturbed, they utter a raspy chatter of irritation, quite unlike their ethe songs. In contrast to their spectacular singing, Palau Bush Warblers are not much to look at. They are olive drab birds whose only prominent markings are a dark line from the bill through the eye, and a eyebrow and crescent below the eye.

The long slender bill is bright orange with a da
line along the top, and the long legs are brow
ish orange. The pattern of color is very similar
that of the Giant White-eye, and the two prese
one of the few identification challenges for bi
ers at Palau. The warbler is an altogether sli
mer and more delicate-looking bird, and the th
bill is distinctive. The Giant White-eye has
dark ear-patch, a complete pale yellow eye ri
that extends behind the eye over the auricula
a much heavier bill, and darker legs. The tv
birds' songs are completely different, but th
scolding chatters can be similar.

Palau Bush warbler nests are domed structur
woven of grasses and leaves, with the entran
on the side, lined with fine plant material (belc
left). They are built low in the crotch of a tree
shrub. The single egg is dark purplish-brown
very unusual color for bird eggs generally. T
incubation and fledgling periods are not know
Begging juveniles are colored just like t
adults. Bush warblers eat small invertebra
such as snails and insects, gleaned from leav
and stems. Pairs are highly territorial, and spa
themselves at intervals in their forest habit
They are common in forest and scrub throug
out Palau from Babeldaob to Peleliu, but a
scarce in mangrove forests.

The Palau Bush warbler belongs to a fam
known as Old World warblers, only two gene
of which are found on islands in the Paci
When first discovered by scientists, the bu
warbler was placed in a genus of its o
(Psamathia) because not enough was known
determine its nearest relatives. However, bas
on research done by HDP and others, we c
be fairly certain that the Palau bird is a clo
relative of bush warblers in the genus Ce
found throughout Eurasia. It is also related
the Shade Warbler C. parens of San Cristoba
the Solomon Islands, and the Fiji Bush Warb
C. vitiensis, which are the only other Cettia w
blers in the tropical Pacific. All members of t
genus have dark-colored eggs, most bu
domed nests, and most have long-sustain
whistles as part of their song. In fact, Japane
birders will note the similarity of the Palau bir
song to that of the Japanese Bush Warbler
diphone. The Palau Bush Warbler is Pala
only endemic with a mainland Eurasian, rat
than Indo- Australian, ancestry.

CITRINE WHITE-EYE/ CHARMBEDEL
Zosterops semperi semperi   Zosterop

L 10 cm, 4 in. White-eyes are so named because most species worldwide have a prominent white
around the eye. The genus name *Zosterops* means "shining eye" in Latin. Palau has three white-eyes
only this one has the eye-ring typical of the family. The English name has changed several times rece
For many years, all of the "typical" white-eyes of Micronesia were considered subspecies of the Br
White-eye, but behavioral studies by HDP and recent DNA research have resulted in the breakup of
"species" into several components. This Palau subspecies, along with similar birds at Chuuk (*owstoni*)
Pohnpei *(takatsukasai)* had the unwieldy name Caroline Islands White-eye until the English Names C
mittee of the International Ornithological Congress (IOC) proposed this simpler one based on the b
yellow-green color. Although the three subspecies look nearly alike, the Palau one has a different call
that heard on the other islands, so the possibility remains that it may eventually prove to be an end
species. That call, a brightly whistled *cheer cheer cheer* is uttered constantly by flocks of Citrine Wh
eyes as they move through the forest canopy. It is similar to the call of the Dusky White-eye with whicl
Citrines often associate, but is a single repeated note rather than a descending series.

Citrine White-eyes move about in flocks of a dozen or more birds, usually fairly high in the trees.
prefer more open forest and edges to the deep forest interior. They feed on small insects picked
leaves and twigs. The flocks only break up when the birds are nesting. The nest is similar to that of c
white-eyes, a smple woven cup suspended in a horizontal fork of a tree branch. Actually, we know very
about the breeding biology of the Citrine White-eye at Palau, despite the fact that it is a common bird
unevenly distributed among the islands from Babeldaob south to the larger Rock Islands, but it is ap
ently absent from Angaur and Peleliu. The best places to look for this species are the Rock islands and
edges of savannahs on southern Babeldaob.

DUSKY WHITE-EYE/ CHETITALIAL
Zosterops finschii   Zosteropic

L 10 cm, 4 in. The Dusky White-eye is unusual in that it entirely lacks the white eye-ring that characteri
this bird family. Instead, the ring of feathers surrounding the eye is dark brownish-gray, just like the
rounding plumage. The eye itself is brownish red, so this bird's name seems a little silly until one kno
the family to which the bird belongs. The Dusky White-eye is easily the plainest and dullest colored of
of Palau's endemics. But what it lacks in color, it makes up in personality. Flocks of up to 15 Dusky Whi
eyes roam the forest canopy throughout Palau, flitting boisterously among the leaves and branches
constantly uttering their characteristic calls. The notes are similar to those of the Citrine White-eye, w
which the Duskies may associate, but grouped in clusters of usually four descending notes accented
the first: *FID-dle-dee-deee*. Visitors from North America will be reminded of the flight call of the Ameri
Goldfinch *Cardeulis tristis*. Flocks fly high over the forest from one feeding site to another, then settle
the tops of the trees and quiet down as they feed on seeds and small fruits such as berries. After a ti
the whole flock may erupt with much clamor and fly off to another tree. Dusky White-eyes are much less
stricted in their habitat choice than Citrine White-eyes, being found in virtually every forest or scrub hab
from Peleliu to Babeldaob (they are not found on Angaur). They are much more likely to inhabit the inte
of deep forests, and on Babeldaob they outnumber the Citrines considerably. Among the Rock Islands,
two species exist in roughly equal numbers.

Although it is placed in the same genus *Zosterops* as the Citrine White-eye, the Dusky is clearly an al
rant member of the group. In fact, its only close relatives are the Gray-brown White-eye *Z. ponapensi*
Pohnpei and the Kosrae White-eye *Z. cinereus*. These are also dull-colored birds, but do have a v
narrow version of the typical eye-ring. All three were once regarded as belonging to the same species,
their vocalizations and behavior are different from island to island and HDP considers them full specie

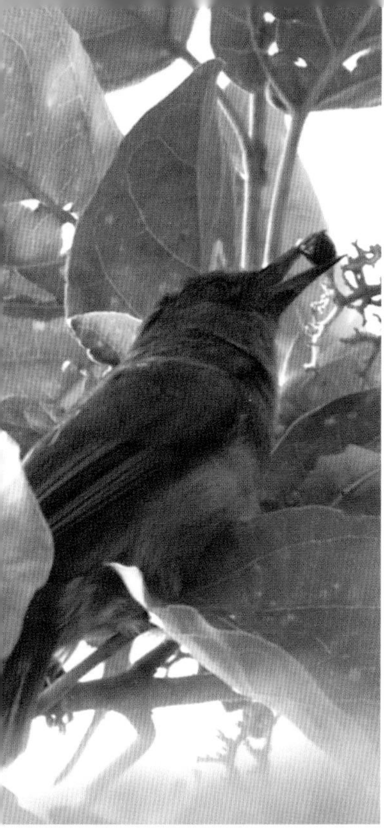

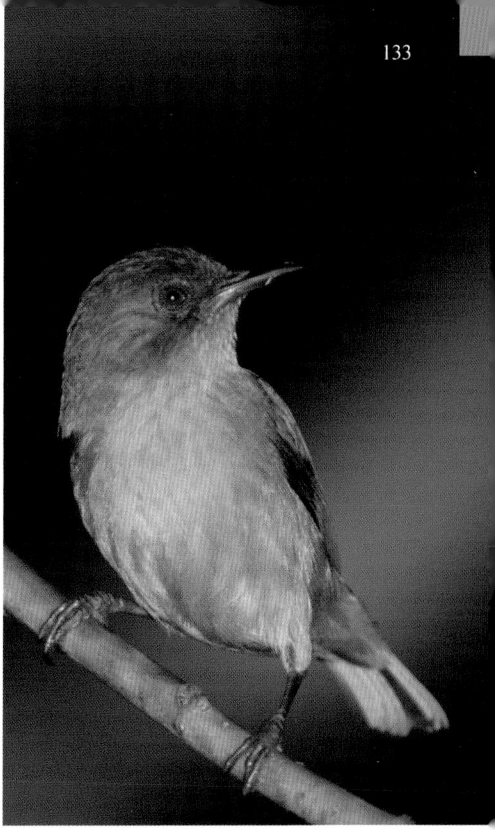

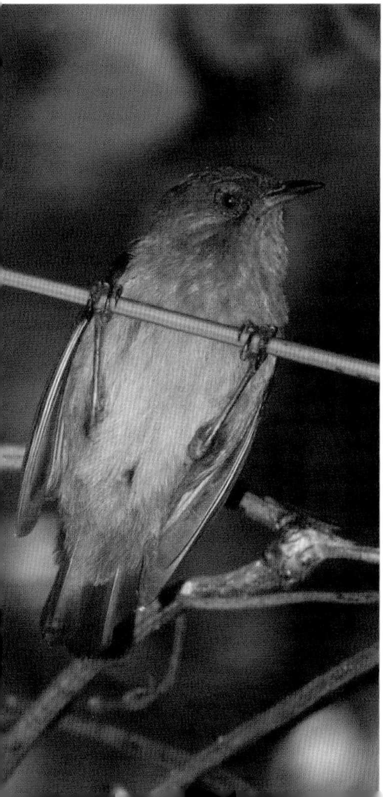

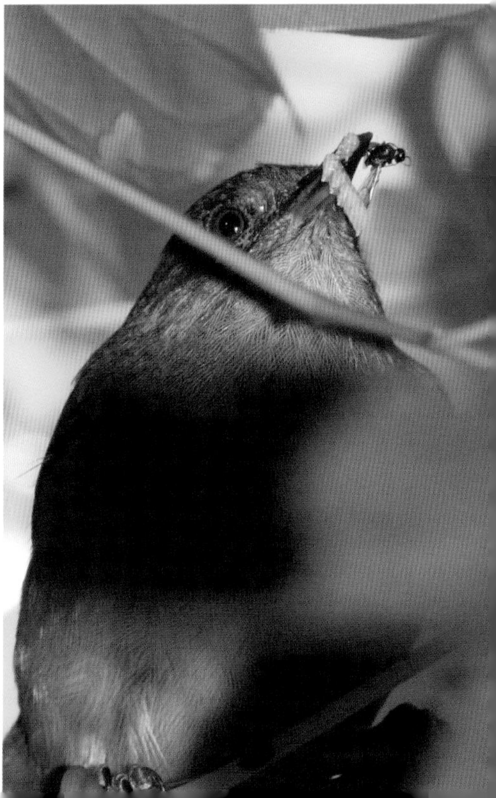

As indicated by some of MTE's recent observations, flocking behavior in Dusky White-eye may even extend into the breeding season. nest she observed on Ulong Island held only two chicks, but was attended by six birds that all looked alike, so she could not tell which two were the actual parents and which were nest helpers. Apparently these birds were engaged in cooperative breeding, a phenomenon that has received a lot of research attention recently. Why would some members of a species forego the opportunity to breed themselves, and help others to do so? Is this truly altruistic behavior? Based on studies of other cooperatively breeding birds worldwide we now know that such behavior is fairly common. In most cases that have been studied, nest helpers turn out to be previous offspring of the nesting pair. So the helpers are helping to raise brothers and sisters, and thus perpetuating some of their own genes. But more importantly, in species with high population density like the Duskies, where territories are not easy to establish or defend, helpers improve their chances of inheriting a territory from their parents and also improve their parenting skills when they do nest on their own. In the long run, the seemingly altruistic behavior is actually in the individual's best interest.

The nest itself is a tightly woven cup or sac suspended from a fork or from crossed vines several meters off the ground, but not in the high canopy. It is made of grass stems, mosses, and other plant fibers. The young are colored much like their parents, and are fed mostly insects and larvae to promote rapid growth, eventhough the adults eat more plant than animal material. Parents, and probably the nest helpers, bring food at intervals of 10-15 minutes, and remove fecal sacs from the nest. (Young birds produce their droppings inside a thin membrane so the parents can pick them up easily and dispose of them away from the nest.) When nests are disturbed, the entire group of parents, helpers and young start a chattering commotion to keep the potential predator away. Studies of other species have shown that pairs with nest helpers consistently fledge more young than pairs without them, but whether that is true of the Dusky White-eye remains to be learned. The breeding biology of this species would be a wonderful research project for a young naturalist.

Juv.

GIANT WHITE-EYE/ CHARMBEDEL
Megazosterops palauensis   Zosteropi

L 14 cm, 5.5 in. The Giant White-eye is perhaps Palau's most important and interesting endemic beca
it represents not only an endemic species, but an endemic genus whose relationships have yet to be de
mined. When a genus contains only one species, it is called monotypic, and *Megazosterops* is an exam
The English name is a translation of the Latin genus name, and even though it is small as birds go, it
giant when compaired to white-eyes in the genus *Zosterops*, such as the Dusky and the Citrine. As in
case of the Dusky, the name white-eye is not really appropriate for the Giant because it lacks the us
white eye-ring. However, it does have a yellow eye-ring that is continuous with a yellow streak behind
eye and over the dusky cheek, giving the bird somewhat the appearance of wearing spectacles. Overa
is mainly olive drab, but with a fairly thick orange-yellow bill tinged brown along the culmen, and e
greenish-gray legs. This color pattern is close to that of the Palau Bush Warbler, which is often found in
same habitat. Note, however, the warbler's much thinner bill, yellow legs, and dark streak through the e
The Giant White-eye lacks dark coloring between the eye and bill and its cheek patches are darker t
the surrounding feathers and faintly streaked.

Despite its size, heavy bill, and other non-white-eye-like features, the Giant behaves like a white-e
roaming the forest in small flocks of about six birds. They feed on adult insects, caterpillars, and f
mostly in the high canopy, but come down into the understory to confront intruders. The birds are noisy
curious, gathering about observers and raising a commotion with their harsh calls that include a dry ra
and an irritating, long-drawn-out *scheeee-e-e-e*. When calling, Giants hold their bill open continuously
vealing a striking orange-yellow mouth lining.

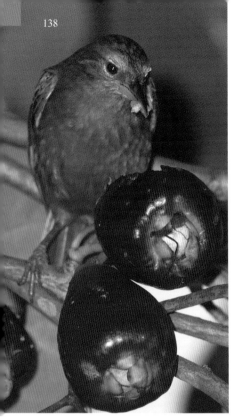

They favor a variety of habitats, from primary fo to secondary scrub, but have a mysteriously pa distribution. They are found only on limestone lands or limestone portions of islands, but not c of them, with some unexplained gaps. They common on the large uninhabited island of Nge tabel (as, for example, on Ngeremdiu beach) on Peleliu. On the latter they are often seen in small **bedel** trees *Macaranga carolinensis* which they are named, as well as in thicket weedy *Leucaena glauca* planted after World W But they are absent from islands between Nge tabel and Peleliu, such as Eil Malk, and nearb lands like Ulong, that seem to be ecologically i tical. Very rarely are they seen in limestone for around Koror and southern Babeldaob. No ex nation for this odd distribution has yet been offe

The most remarkable thing about this bird i song. White-eyes are not noted as vocalists, this one is an exception, and the song coulc considered one of the world's most unusual. exceptionally loud for such a relatively small and parts of it can even be heard over the sour an outboard engine as one cruises around Nge tabel. A single bird can sound like a chorus.

most far-carrying notes are slurred whistles
initially go down the scale *peeer-peeer-peeer*
squeezed-out quality as if uttered with great
This is followed by a swelling trill over which
rd sings upslurred whistles *wheep! wheep!*
o! At close range, one can hear, underlying
histles, a mechanical-sounding rhythmic rattle
king sound like that of pebbles or shells being
aged in the hand. The performance also has
t starts and stops, as if turned on and off. The
chorus at Peleliu can be almost deafening.

est of the Giant White-eye has never been
ved, despite the fact that the bird is common
st on Peleliu. MTE recently photographed a
fledged family group at Ngeremdiu beach,
oung birds still being fed by their parents, but
not find the nest itself. Fledglings look like the
. Study of its breeding habits would be an im-
t contribution to determining what exactly
nigmatic bird is. Some authors have sug-
d that it may not actually be a white-eye. But
zosterops would be an oddball in whatever
it was placed, and for now white-eyes are as
a guess as any for its relationships. DNA
s are clearly needed to resolve the issue.

Juv. 139

MICRONESIAN STARLING/ KIUID
Aplonis opaca orii   Sturnic

L 23 cm, 9 in. The noisy and conspicuous Micronesian Starling is well known throughout Micronesia, and each of the major island groups in the region has its own slightly different subspecies. The starlings are easy to identify in most places, as at Palau, because they are usually the only all-black songbird prese. The adults have glossy plumage with purple and green reflections, and piercing yellow eyes that stand against the dark feathering as if lighted from within. Young birds have dull sooty brown plumage, with prominent pale streaks underneath. Their eyes are brown at first, but turn yellow before the streaky plu age is replaced (below).

Although they make a lot of vocal noise, Micronesian starlings cannot really be considered singers. T most common call is a harsh rolling *brleeep*, but they have a variety of loud whistles, squeaks, and gurg notes that never seem to be organized into anything worthy of being called a song. Many of the notes h an irritatingly dissonant or screechy quality. These calls can be used to defend territories, but also se as beacons to assemble raiding parties at seabird colonies. They are often seen in small to large floc the former often called family groups, but they can also be found as singles or pairs. Starlings are disli by most other birds and even some people because they are aggressive and pushy, and often gang up other species. Smaller birds sometimes harass starlings (probably with good reason, see next pages), Palauan boys like to take pot-shots at them with air guns (although this is illegal). In earlier times, starli were highly regarded as a food item by both Palauans and Japanese residents, and were hunted for purpose, so they have learned to keep their distance from people. Despite hunting pressure, the Micro sian Starling maintains its position as the most abundant Palauan bird.

Although they live in all terrestrial habitats, Micro
sian Starlings are mainly found in disturbed ar
and forests rather than the deep forest. Such h
tats increased greatly during the Japanese
before World War II, when much Palauan forest
cleared for agriculture, and the starlings increa
greatly. Observers at the time reported flocks o
to 50 birds, but the usual flock size today is
5-30 birds. They fly high in the air, and cover l
distances between islands.

Pairs of Micronesian Starlings are very aggres
in defense of their nests, driving away all other b
and even sizable monitor lizards that come
close. The nest is built in a tree cavity, with pa
being favored. The nest is made of leaves, par
nus stems, grasses, and pieces of palm fronds
often protrude through the mouth of the nest h
The larger materials are changed fairly often du
the nest cycle. The two or three eggs are a beau
sky blue with large purple spots. Surprisingly
such a common bird, very little detail is known a
the length of incubation or nestling periods.

Much of the Micronesian Starlings' bad reputat[ion] results from their habit of stealing eggs. They ha[ve] heavy bills with a sharp hook at the tip, and [can] easily break even fairly large eggs such as thos[e] noddies and other seabirds. Their predilection [for] eggs is surprising because their diet otherwise [is] mostly fruits and insects. Around a nesting colo[ny] starlings hang out until a bird leaves its egg un[at]tended and then move in to devour it. Sometim[es] one bird will call in reinforcements to try to haras[s a] bird off its egg. Surprisingly, once an egg hatch[es] the starlings are no longer a danger and are [not] known to kill nestlings. Perhaps they just view e[ggs] as another kind of fruit! But even their fruit diet g[ets] them into trouble with farmers because of [the] damage they do to crops like papayas. Their love [of] large fruits also brings them in conflict with fruit b[ats] but the much larger bats usually win the squabb[le] and the starlings have to settle for scraps. The s[tar]lings feed mostly high in the forest canopy rat[her] than near the ground.

BLUE-FACED PARROT-FINCH
Erythrura trichroa pelewensis

Estrildi

L 11 cm, 4.5 in. This beautiful little bird, despite its rich coloring, is not well known at Palau, and appare
does not even have a Palauan name. It is a tiny, dark-colored bird that feeds mostly high in the trees
makes sounds that are easily overlooked among those of insects. The plumage is a rich dark green,
a well-defined dark blue mask in the face, and a crimson rump and tail. The folded tail feathers come
sharp point. The heavy bill is black throughout. The Blue-faced Parrot-Finch is widespread from eastern
donesia to Melanesia and northern Australia. In Micronesia, it is found on Chuuk, Pohnpei, and Kosrae
well as Palau. For many years, the Palau population was known only from one specimen collected on
beldaob and described by Japanese ornithologists in the 1920s. By the 1970s, it was considered poss
extinct, and it was included in the first list of Endangered Species for the Trust Territory of the Pacific
lands. When HDP and co-workers visited in 1976, they found a flock of 6 on Arakebesang, the first sigh
in half a century! The same team finally discovered the key to finding this bird at Palau: ***ngas***, or ironw
trees *Casuarina equisetifolia*. Also important is knowing the bird's call, which sounds like at least two
sects common in the islands. It is a faint, high-pitched metallic *tink* similar to the sound of two coins clic
together. Now that we know where to look and what to listen for, the Blue-faced Parrot-Finch turns ou
be not so rare as it is inconspicuous, and fairly easily found with a little searching. Since the 1970s, t
have been found to be widespread but in low numbers from Peleliu to southern Babeldaob. The first si
ing on Babeldaob since the original specimen was a bird seen by HDP in 1978, and a few were spo
there also by others, but the main population seems to be centered in the Rock Islands. In the 2005
survey sponsored by the Palau Conservation Society, a small flock was found on Koror in an isolated gr
of *Casuarina* trees right outside the PCS office, where HDP spotted them again in 2007. MTE has b
seeing small flocks of 3-5 birds in fig trees around her house on Koror since 1994, a few times a year w
there are ripe figs. All photos shown here taken on Koror.

Juv.

At Palau, Blue-faced Parrot-Finches seem to s\
cialize on only two kinds of trees. They eat *Cas*
rina seeds, which they skillfully extract from
hard "cones" and also often feed on ripe figs (*F*
sp.), such as those that grow around MTE's ho
on Koror, where these photos were taken.

To date, these are the only trees in which they h
been observed feeding at Palau, but on other
lands, their food preferences are not so specific
Chuuk and Kosrae they prefer low shrubs
dense vines near the ground rather than the ca
pies of tall trees. Elsewhere, they feed mostly
grass seeds, including those of bamboo. And t
may be nomadic, following the fruiting season
preferred seed plants. There is some evidence
they are also nomadic on Palau, moving along
lands to search for fruiting figs and mature *Cas*
rina cones.

Nothing is known of the nesting habits of the Bl
faced Parrot-Finch at Palau. At Chuuk, the
itself is a bulky structure of coarse plant mate
with an entrance in the side, and the birds lay
dull white eggs.

Juv.

e nest is usually placed in a tree, often the top of ɔalm or Pandanus. Parrot-finches at Chuuk netimes nest in holes in cliffs or even in the wall aves, sometimes quite far from the entrance. If auan birds have similar habits, it might explain / they are most commom in the Rock Islands, ere such sites would be available.

E's photos shown here are the first documenta- of the juvenile and transitional plumages of the au bird. Juveniles (left and right) are duller and uniformly green than adults, with subdued red e rump and tail, a yellowish belly, and no blue sk. The bill is orange, blotched irregularly with k. As the birds mature (below), the orange as are gradually replaced by black, the other rs brighten, and the blue mask appears, ill- ned at first. The orange bill color of the juvenile not been reported in other populations, and be a distinctive feature of the Palau subspe- . Other populations of Blue-faced Parrot-Finch e inconspicuous songs, but none has been de- bed or heard from any of the Micronesian ones. t is not to say they have no song, because it d easily have been overlooked.

BLACK-HEADED MUNIA/ KANARIA
Lonchura malacca   Estrildid

L 11 cm, 4.5 in. This attractive little finch is popular in the cage bird trade, and the Palau population pr
ably descended from pet birds released after World War II. It was first officially reported in the islands
1951, and has now become abundant around Koror and on southern Babeldaob. It lives in open gra
areas such as roadsides, so it is familiar to most Palauans. It is also noticable for its flocking behavior
the 1980s, flocks of 5-30 birds were reported, but flock size has increased greatly since then and too
huge hordes, some numbering in the 100s, of these tiny birds can be seen around the Koror landfill a
the Babeldaob road during the nonbreeding season. When nesting, the big flocks break up, but the bi
still are usually seen in smaller groups rather than as single birds or pairs. The members of a flock utte
high-pitched short *tee* or *dee* call as they fly, but they are not noisy because the notes are very qu
Sometimes these notes are organized into a weak song, but Black-headed Munias are not noted for th
voices, perhaps because some of the notes are outside the range of human hearing.

Adult Black-headed Munias, as the name says, have a dark brownish black head and chest and a bl
belly, while the rest of the plumage is a rich reddish chestnut. The pale blue bill is proportionately very la
and heavy for cracking hard grass seeds. Based on these plumage characters, the Palau population
longs to the subspecies *L.m.jagori* found in the Philippines, Borneo, and Sulawesi. It has been introdu
to many places around the world, including Guam, Okinawa, and Hawaii. Interestingly, a different spec
the Scaly-breasted Munia *Lonchura punctulata* was introduced to Palau before the Black-headed (an
still common today on Yap). It was reported to be well established on southern Babeldaob in 1949. H
ever, it has not been reported since then, and apparently was displaced by the Black-headed Munia,
cause the habitats available in Palau could not support two very similar species. The Palauan nam
based on the Spanish word *Canaria* for canary, and was probably picked up from Chamorro speakers
Guam who use that name for the Black-headed Munia there.

Young birds begin life with plain dusty-brown p age, paler and buffy below, and a black bill. coloring is obtained gradually over a perio weeks. The nest is quite large for such a small It is a bulky domed cup made of grasses, t and pandanus leaves with an entrance on the It is placed in low shrubbery or grasses. When structing a nest, Black-headed Munias can be flying with long streamers of grass many time: length of the bird itself. The clutch is 4-7 eggs. fledglings still return to the nest at night to slee gether with one adult for several days. Pa continue to feed the chicks for several weeks they learn to forage for themselves.

In most previous literature on Palau birds, this cies was known in English as the Chestnut M. kin, and elsewhere it has been called various combinations. In an effort to standardize usage English Names Committee of the Internationa nithological Congress recommends the u here, and eliminates the name "mannikin" from names altogether.

153

Juv.

EASTERN YELLOW WAGTAIL
Motacilla tschutschensis

Motacilli

L 17 cm, 6.5 in. The Eastern Yellow Wagtail is a regular winter resident in low numbers at Palau, but it was not reported officially from the islands until the 1970s. Whether they were simply overlooked before th we cannot say. It used to be considered part of the Yellow Wagtail species, which has recently been into Western *M. flava* and Eastern species. Most, if not all, of the birds seen at Palau appear to belon the subspecies *M.t.semillima* which breeds on the Kamchatka Peninsula of Russia. Eastern Yellow W tails live in open areas where they often perch and run on the ground. At Palau, they can be seen on letic fields, runways, and lawns. The greatest concentration is found around the Koror landfill. They slender, long-tailed birds that feed mostly on insects. When they arrive in September or October, they mostly in their basic plumage, plain white below, gray above with a bold white streak over the eye. C the next 6-7 months, they acquire their alternate, or breeding plumage with bright yellow underparts an green back, which contrasts with the gray crown. Molting birds can look rather blotchy. The call is a ring *tsweep*.

Two other species of Wagtail have been observed at Palau as rare visitors. **The Gray Wagtail** *M. cine* is similar to the Eastern Yellow, but larger, with a longer tail. It never shows green on the back, and yellow of the underparts does not extend into the throat. Females have white throats, males black. In fli these show a single bold white stripe and a yellow rump. The **White Wagtail** *M. alba* has been seen tv at Palau. It is entirely gray and white, with the entire forehead, face, and throat white, and a black patc the chest. In the same family with the wagtails are streaky brown birds called pipits. The **Red-throa Pipit** *Anthus cervinus* is heavily streaked below and usually has a pale brick-red tinge in the throat. It been seen several times at Palau. The larger **Richard's Pipit** *A. richardi* was recently photographee Eric VanderWerf at the Malakal Sewage Ponds. It is less heavily streaked, and lacks any red tinge in throat. (all four are shown on p. 157)

GALLERY OF RARITIES

On these pages we present an arbitrary selection of birds that have been documented for Palau, but wh
are truly the rarest of the rare. Some of them may be found here again, others may not. None of them a
regular visitors, but some show up every few years, like the Blue Rock Thrush (next page, bottom), wh
has been spotted in the same area on Koror by MTE every few years since 1994. How do such birds g
to Palau? Occasionally, birds are disorientated for a variety of reasons and appear in unexpected plac
Sometimes north-south migrants overshoot the usual destinations and appear further north or south th
normal. Birds that normally migrate down the east Asian coast through Taiwan and the Philippines m
wander too far east and end up at Palau. Birders consider these rare visitors the "crown jewels" of birdi
Several of the records represented here have not yet been properly published in scientific journals, but
could not resist this opportunity to share them with readers of this book. Proper publication will follow. T
quality of these photos varies strikingly, since some species have only been recorded here with a sin
photograph so far, or have been recorded but yet to be photographed at Palau.

Gray Wagtail (*Motacilla cinerea*)

Paul Pisano

White Wagtail (*Motacilla alba*)

Martin Hale

Oriental Reed Warbler (*Acrocephalus orientalis*)

Paul Pisano

Siberian Rubythroat (*Luscinia calliope*)

Michelle & Peter Wong

Richard's Pipit (*Anthus richardi*)

Eric VanderWerf

Red-throated Pipit (*Anthus cervinus*)

Martin Hale

n Shrike (*Lanius cristatus*)

Brown Hawk-Owl (*Ninox scutulata*) at Helen Island

Helen Reef Conservation Officer Homar

Michelle & Peter Wong

rowed Thrush (*Turdus obscurus*)

Scaly Thrush (*Zoothera dauma*) at Rock Island beach.

© Martin Hale

Rock Thrush (*Monticola solitarius*; female) t: taken on Koror, in a limestone cave at night.

BIRDS OF PONDS AND WETLANDS

Freshwater habitats are important to birds worldwide, and are often scarce on islands. Palau has only a few natural freshwater lakes, and has flowing streams only on Babeldaob. A few of the Rock Islands are known for their marine lakes, but these do not harbor birds that are not well adapted to salt water. Consequently, birds that depend on ponds and lakes, such as the Pacific Black Duck, Common Moorhen, and Purple Swamphen, have historically been scarce at Palau. However, human activities have increased the number and extent of freshwater wetlands, to the benefit especially of migratory visitors. Reservoirs, taro patches, aquaculture ponds, sewage treatment ponds, rain pools in landfills, and even bomb craters from World War II have increased the availability of such habitats. Some of the birds in this section, such as the Pacific Reef Heron, are equally at home in fresh and salt water, but tend to feed in saltwater areas mainly at low tide when large flats are exposed. Some species in this section, while usually considered wetland birds, may also be found sometimes in dry habitats far from water. Three main bird groupings, **herons**, **egrets**, and **bitterns** Ardeidae, **rails** and their relatives Rallidae and **ducks** Anatidae, are covered here with the exception of one rail (Slaty-legged Crake) that is grouped with the forest birds. Herons and egrets are long-legged and long-necked birds that fly with the neck tucked back in an S-curve (as contrasted with shorebirds and rails, which fly with the neck straight out) and the legs extended. Herons tend to be dark colored, bitterns tend to be brown with streaks, and egrets tend to be white, but there are exceptions to these rather arbitrary categories. Similarly, rails tend to have long bills, while crakes have short ones. Both are chickenlike birds most often found in wet habitats. The related moorhen is a swimmer that resembles a duck except for its pointed bill. The number of individuals as well as species of wintering ducks has increased in Palau recently, and probably more would be seen if people would stop harassing them with air guns and noise.

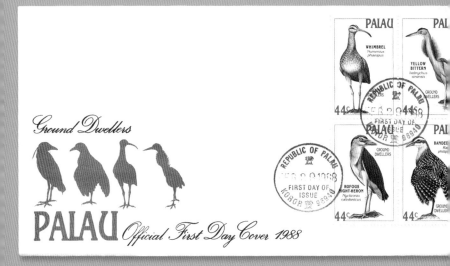

RUFOUS NIGHT HERON/ MELABAOB
Nycticorax caledonicus pelewensis   Arde■

L 58 cm, 23 in. Rufous Night Herons are found from the Philippines to Australia and eastern Melane
Palau and Chuuk in Micronesia share a distinctive subspecies named for Palau. The different subspe
vary considerably among themselves in plumage color. The Palau birds are among the darker varia
being a rich reddish or maroon-brown color. Australian birds are much brighter and paler, especially or
neck, and used to be called Nankeen, rather than Rufous, Night Heron. Both terms are color names
often used in everyday English. These handsome herons are found from Angaur to Babeldaob, m■
along coastlines, and are less likely than other herons to be seen at inland ponds or wetlands. They
to congregate near good feeding sites. Small groups perch or roost in trees such as mangroves during
day, usually returning to the same favored spot day after day. They fly out to tidal flats to feed at dawn
into the night. Their flight is direct, with relatively slow wing beats, similar to that of a fruit bat. They
almost any kind of small animal they can catch, including lizards, fish, and even smaller birds. They
stealth hunters, often sitting motionless for long periods, watching for the movement of potential prey. A
concentration of Rufous Night Herons can be found at the Koror landfill, where they probably catch
and mice or other vermin attracted by the garbage, and they seem not at all disturbed by the human ac
nearby. On the other hand, Palauan villagers dislike night herons because they are said to take baby c■
ens. When forced to fly, they utter a loud *kwok*. This sound is also made at night by birds flying overh■

They usually nest in small colonies, in trees near water. The nests are from 2-5 m. above the groun■
water, as may be the case) and hold 1-3 pale blue eggs. Nests have been reported throughout the se■
half of the year, but none have been studied in detail, so we know very little about the breeding biolo■
this species at Palau. This heron is closely related to the Black-crowned Night Heron, which is ra■
Palau. Juveniles of the two species are heavily streaked with dull brown, and can be difficult to tell ap■

Juv.

Immature

BLACK-CROWNED NIGHT HERON
Nycticorax nycticorax   Ardei

L 64 cm, 25 in. The Black-crowned Night Heron is often referred to as a cosmopolitan species becau
is found almost worldwide except for Australasia, including the Hawaiian Islands. In Micronesia, it is on
rare nonbreeding visitor. Based on recent observations, a few individuals may be present at Palau e
year. Adults, with their distinctive black, gray, and white plumage and blood-red eyes are easily di
guished from their more common cousin, the Rufous Night Heron. Juvenile birds are a different matter
veniles of both species are heavily streaked with dull brown, including the crown, and both can have ye
eyes, but the Black-crown have usually more gray, the Rufous more rust coloring. At Palau, the best di
guishing feature is the eye color, which, by the time a young Black-crown is old enough to fly to Palau ('
do not breed there) should show a tinge of the red color it will achieve as an adult (below). The imma
or subadult second-year plumage of the Black-crowned Night Heron, which has not yet been reporte
Palau, is quite different from that of the Rufous. It lacks streaks entirely and looks much like the adult
the black and gray replaced by brown and light brown, with an orange eye. The photo of the adult be
were taken at the Koror landfill, the juvenile at the Malakal sewer ponds.

Two other night herons have been recorded once each many years ago at Palau, and both could easil
confused with the Rufous Night Heron, but both are smaller, with much shorter bills. The **Japanese N
Heron** *Goisachius goisagi* is dark chestnut overall, including the crown, and shows a bold band of t
across the open wing. The **Malayan Night Heron** *G. melanolophus* is similar but with a black crown
white tips to the primaries and primary coverts. Whether these rare birds will turn up at Palau aga
anyone's guess.

Juv.

RAY HERON
dea cinerea   **V**
                                                      Ardeidae

17 cm, 46 in. Although the Gray Heron is widespread and common throughout Africa and Eurasia east the Philippines and Indonesia, it was not officially recorded in Micronesia until the late 1980s. Since n, these large graceful birds have turned up irregularly but fairly often in the Marianas, Yap and Palau. e first hypothetical sightings at Palau was one in the 1970s, and HDP saw another one in 1988. The spes was confirmed for Palau by Eric VanderWerf who photographed one at Peleliu in 2006. The Gray ron is the largest heron likely to be seen at Palau, mostly gray with a noticeable yellow bill and a black eak through the eye extended into a long head plume. In flight, the primaries and secondaries are noably darker than the rest of the wing, a useful mark at a distance (below, right). The pictures below of ifferent individuals were taken by MTE in January 2008 at the Malakal sewer.

RIATED HERON
torides striatus   **V**
                                                      Ardeidae

6 cm, 18 in. The two herons on this page represent the size extremes in the family, but both are mainly n gray and black birds. Juveniles of this species are heavily streaked (=striated) on the neck with dark wn. Like the much larger Gray Heron, this is a rare visitor to Palau, but is possibly present every year ery low numbers. It has become a fairly regular visitor in recent years to the Mariana Islands and Yap, well as Palau, where it has been spotted near the aquarium, and in taro patches. It is an odd-looking l for a heron, often perching in trees with its neck tucked in. When alarmed, it assumes a more heron- stance, with the long neck extended. It may utter a loud squawk as it takes flight. Striated Herons ong to a species complex that has a nearly worldwide distribution.

Michelle & Peter Wong

YELLOW BITTERN/
CHELOTEACHEL

Ixobrychus sinensis   Arde

L 38 cm, 15 in. Bitterns are a subgroup of he
usually characterized by streaked plumage
stealthy habits. The Yellow Bittern, formerly c
Chinese Least Bittern, is a small, sandy-col
heron that lives in freshwater habitats such as
patches, ponds, and swamps, as well as
grasslands and weedy places far from wate
moves very slowly in tall grass stalking its s
animal prey, and may freeze, pointing its long
skyward, making the bird nearly impossible to
among the grass stems. It is difficult to flush, ar
flight is slow and clumsy, with legs dangling. In
tained flight, it may utter a double-noted squ
kak-kak. It also utters a scratchy *creek* and a
croak, which are considered a bad omen v
heard near a house in Palau. Except when nes
Yellow Bitterns are solitary birds. They breed
the Seychelles through southern and eastern As
northern Melanesia and western Micronesia. N
ern populations are migratory, and some of the
seen at Palau may be migrants from Asia.

Adult male Yellow Bitterns have a dark cap,
buff (sometimes with pinkish tints) neck with s
faint streaking on the foreneck, pale buff underp
and a reddish brown hindneck and back with ma
tinges. females lack the maroon and have re
brown streaks on the neck and back. In flight,
sexes show big flashing buffy patches contra
with the dark flight feathers. Immatures resemb
males but are more heavily streaked, includin
wing patches. Yellow Bitterns usually nest in
colonies, but in Micronesia nests may be so
Breeding biology has not been studied at Palau
presumably it is similar to that observed on G
where the nest is built in thick grasses or some
in trees over fresh water. It is a platform of gra
or twigs with vegetation interlaced over it to fo
canopy. Three or four pale greenish blue eggs
a clutch. The incubation period is about 2.5 w
and complete fledging takes more than 2 week
One other small bittern has been recorded
(1931) from Palau. The **Von Schrenk's Bi**
I.eurhythmus is patterned like the Yellow Bitter
is dark chestnut on the upper parts, with grayis
wing patches.

The photos shown were all taken in Airai State.

PACIFIC REEF HERON
SECHOU
Egretta sacra   Ardeic

L 58 cm, 23 in. The Pacific Reef Heron is the m
widespread and familiar member of its family in
tropical Pacific, being found from the coasts of ea
ern and southeastern Asia to New Zealand and
nearly all the islands of Polynesia and Microne
except for Hawaii. It is found throughout the isla
of Palau. It has two main color forms, or morphs, a
a rare intermediate one. The dark morph is d
slaty gray with greenish legs and a mostly dark
while the white morph is all white with yellow l
and bill (with a dark culmen). Intermediates
highly variable, but usually mostly white, blotch
spotted, and streaked with slaty gray. The interm
ates are uncommon, representing only about
percent of the birds seen in Micronesia, while
ratio of dark to white birds is about 60:40. The c
forms interbreed freely, and many mixed pairs
seen. At Palau, dark reef herons are easily identi
by their color, but white birds can be easily confu
with white egrets of several species, and the
lauan name *Sechou* is used for all. Compared
most egrets, reef herons are shorter-legged
generally chunkier, with a proportionally m
heavier bill.

Pacific Reef Herons favor exposed reefs and
flats for feeding, but they may also forage aro
freshwater ponds and streams inland. There is s
evidence that white birds feed more in the surf, w
dark birds more often stalk the flats, apparentl
match their color to the substrate and thus rec
their visibility. When stalking prey, they assum
distinctive horizontal posture with the body held
to the ground, quite unlike the upright posture
other herons. They eat mostly fish and crustace
especially crabs. Sometimes they hunt on a be
where they wait for small fish being chased by la
fish to strand themselves out of the water. Out o
frying pan, into the fire! Sometimes they steal ch
from the nests of seabirds, and terns someti
mob them as they would any other predator. O
foods include insects and lizards. Pacific
Herons are solitary birds, and territorial in their f
ing areas, but if food is abundant, they may cor
gate in one spot. Next page, bottom: an unu
photo with all three color morphs standing toge
taken at Ngiwal State.

168

H.Douglas Pratt

They build a rather untidy nest of sticks and g
a tree, on the ground, or even on rock ledge
the shore. They nest year-round, but favor t
months. The 2-5 greenish blue eggs hatch in
weeks, with both parents incubating. The
fledge in about 7 weeks.

Reef Herons at Palau are often chased and a
by Collared Kingfishers when competing for
reef flats. The kingfishers will dive down
herons and pick at the top of their head o
over again, until they don't have any feathers
even bleeding (left, middle).

Below an adult white Pacific Reef Heron with
mature dark birds much smaller in size. This
was taken at the Ngatpang aquaculture pon
photos on the next page show typical feeding
ior of a white Pacific Reef Heron, these phot
taken at Carp Island.

CATTLE EGRET/ KEREMLAL SECHOU
Bubulcus ibis coromandus   Ardeid

L 51 cm, 20 in. The Cattle Egret is named for its habit of following livestock and catching the insects th
disturb. Nowadays, they often follow man-made "livestock" such as mowing machines and tractors. T
species evolved in Africa, following the great herds of wild grazers, but during the late 19th and 20th cer
ries, Cattle Egrets underwent a worldwide expansion that took them into the Americas, Eurasia, and A
tralasia. In the 1950s, the species was known only as a rare winter visitor to Palau, but numbers increa
and by 1978 a couple dozen birds remained through the year. Breeding is now suspected, but has ye
be confirmed anywhere in Micronesia. Whether visitor or resident, Cattle Egrets are by far the most num
ous of the white egrets at Palau, and are found throughout the country including the Southwest Islan
Construction of the new capital and Compact Road on Babeldaob have greatly increased the kind of ha
tat these birds prefer, so further increases are likely. More than a hundred birds hang around the Ko
landfill and roost in nearby mangroves. For foraging, Cattle Egrets avoid saltwater habitats and inde
seem to prefer dry places such as runways, roadsides, and lawns. In Palau's more remote islands, th
live around villages, apparently using humans the same way they do cattle! They also use themselves
"beaters", as when a large group works through a field. They walk with a peculiar head-pumping gait, a
may use run-and-stab techniques or even aerial sallies (flycatching) to capture prey. They eat almost
tirely insects. Cattle Egrets are the smallest of the white egrets, and have a short-necked look. Feather
the throat extend almost half way out the bill, giving the bird a distinctive profile. Non-breeding Ca
Egrets are all white with black legs and a yellow bill. In March and April, they begin to acquire their breed
colors including yellow legs as well as bill, brownish orange plumes on the back and foreneck, and
same color nearly covering the entire head (below). The vividness and extent of the color indicates t
Palau birds belong to the eastern Asian subspecies. At the peak of the breeding cycle, the bill and I
briefly turn almost red, and birds seen would be circumstantial evidence that local breeding is taking pla

OTHER WHITE EGRETS

In addition to the Cattle Egret and the white Pa
Reef Heron, three species of white egrets ca
seen at Palau. They migrate to the islands from
in low numbers every year. They tend to congre
around freshwater ponds, when their stepwise
hierarchy is readily apparent (see photo below ta
at the Malakal sewage ponds). The smallest (6
and now most common at Palau is the **Little E**
Egretta garzetta which is about the size of a C
Egret, but much more delicate, with a slender r
It has a thin black bill, gray lores, black legs, a
yellow feet (toes). It is the only egret at Palau
both bill and legs black. First-year Little Egrets
some yellow at the base of the bill and dark gree
legs (left). Somewhat larger (78;28) is the **Yell
billed Egret** *E. intermedia*, formerly called Inte
diate Egret, with a yellow bill, black legs and
and a graceful s-curved neck. Still larger (95;3
the **Great Egret** *Ardea alba* with similar bill an
colors and a characteristic kink in the neck.

Distinguishing the larger two from each other
from non-breeding Cattle Egrets can be a chall
when they are not seen together, especially in f
but note the extremely long legs of the Great E
and the quicker wing beats and short legs o
Cattle (also usually in flocks). Yellow-billed E
prefer drier habitats such as the savannahs of s
ern Babeldaob, but all four white egrets can be
together in some areas like the Malakal s
ponds, with the occasional addition of a white
heron! With a little practice, one can identify the

chelle & Peter Wong

Douglas Pratt

Top: Great Egret

Left: Yellow-billed Egret

Below: Little Egret

Bottom: Cattle Egrets

BUFF-BANDED RAIL/ TERIID
Gallirallus philippensis pelewensis

Rallie

L 31 cm, 12 in. The Buff-banded Rail is a widespread species in the Indo-Pacific region, from the Ph
pines southeast to New Zealand and east to Samoa. In Micronesia, it is found only at Palau, whose
demic subspecies is one of 22 that differ in minor ways but look more or less alike. The plumage is hea
barred below with pale gray and black, and across the chest is a band of buff, also more or less barred
black. On the dorsal side, birds are olive brown with obvious black and white spots, and the upper b
continues the barred pattern of the underparts. The throat, foreneck, and eyebrow stripe are plain gray
contrast neatly with a reddish chestnut crown, nape, and broad eye stripe. When the wing is spread, a
defensive behavior (below), stretching or sunning, the primaries and secondaries show bold brown
rusty-orange bands.

Buff-banded Rails are shy and secretive, but occasionally come into full view along roadsides or in c
fields, especially after rain. They can fly, but prefer to run when frightened. They bathe in roadside pudc
but are easily spooked and run away with the head held low, sometimes uttering a sharp *skeek!* John E
bring reports that Palauans have a saying "**kekora melechol teriid**" that is directed at children who ba
too quickly, comparing them to the rail. Buff-banded Rails often sun themselves with wings open
drooped down at the sides (right, bottom). Their favored habitats are swamps, taro patches, abando
farms, and brushy areas with dense cover. They are found throughout Palau in such places, including
Southwest Islands, but are absent from the Rock Islands where proper habitat does not exist. They
most frequently seen along roadsides in Airai on southern Babeldaob, and they are particularly comm
on Angaur and Peleliu. They have an omnivorous diet that includes insects, snails, seeds, roots, buds,
other plant matter, but they apparently do not damage crops. They occasionally hang out with dome
chickens and share their food. Members of a foraging pair may call back and forth from dense vegeta

At Palau, Buff-banded Rails nest in the last third [of] the year. The nest is a basket or cup of grass built [on] the ground in dense vegetation (left), with stems [in]terlaced over it for concealment. One nest observ[ed] by MTE was only about 5m away from the main ro[ad] on Koror. This nest held 3 eggs, white with redd[ish] brown spots, which is a smaller clutch than repor[ted] elsewhere. Both sexes are reported to incubate, a[nd] because they look alike, it is difficult for an obser[ver] to tell which is doing what. The incubation perio[d is] about 3 weeks. The Koror nest had two entranc[es] and when MTE approached within 40 feet, the in[cu]bating bird would sneak out the backside. Once [the] first egg hatched, the male assumed the role [of] guardian of the nest. Rail chicks are precocial a[nd] nidifugous, meaning they are able to run about a[nd] leave the nest shortly after hatching. In the case [of] this particular nest, only one of the eggs hatch[ed] and when the other 2 failed to do so the same d[ay] as they should, the parents and chick abandon[ed] the nest. Birds can tell when eggs are infertile [be]cause they can hear the young bird inside a live e[gg].

Buff-banded Rail chicks are covered with bla[ck] down except for a bare patch of gray skin around [the] eye. The bill is pink at first. The chick shown in [the] nest still has its white egg tooth, a projection on [the] top of the bill with which the bird breaks out of [the] shell. The tooth drops off almost as soon as [the] chick leaves the nest. In this case, the chick w[as] called from the nest by the parents and escorted i[nto] dense vegetation. Chicks are fed by their paren[ts,] mostly the female, for up to a week until they be[gin] foraging on their own, and they are closely attend[ed] until they are fully grown. They remain all black [at] first, with the bill darkening (middle, right), but so[on] molt into the juvenile plumage that mimics the adu[lt] color pattern, but is less colorful (lower, right). [The] whole process takes about 6 weeks.

COMMON MOORHEN/ DEBAR
Gallinula chloropus

E

Ralli«

L 33 cm, 13 in. Except for its absence from Australia and New Guinea, the Common Moorhen coul« called cosmopolitan in its distribution. In Micronesia, it is found in the Mariana Islands, Yap, and Palau. population at Palau is very small, so the English name is misleading; this is one of the most severely dangered species in the islands. It requires freshwater ponds with little disturbance for reproduction, few of those are present. The largest number (50+) survive on Lake Ngardok on Babeldaob, and fe than 20 inhabit ponds on Angaur. They formerly lived on Koror and Peleliu. Their continued surviva Palau depends on preservation of these few ponds and protection of the birds from illegal hunting. cause moorhens are usually seen swimming, many observers confuse them with ducks, and indeed Palauan name is the same for both. But moorhen bills are very different from those of ducks, and their are not webbed. The bill comes to a sharp point like that of a chicken, and extends back onto the forel as a frontal shield. The plumage is almost entirely dark slate gray, with a line of white edging the flanks bold white lateral undertail coverts that are made more obvious when the bird cocks its tail up, as it c does. The bill and frontal shield are bright red except for a yellow tip, and the legs and feet are yellow red "garters" at the upper end. Immature birds (below, photo taken at Airai puddle) have plain yellow with no frontal shield and somewhat paler body plumage. Such birds were photographed by MTE in 2 in Airai State and Lake Ngardok, indicating that the colony is still reproducing. Moorhens are well ada| to walking on land, but at Palau usually only do so in places out of sight of humans. They have a pec head-pumping gait and seldom fly, but when they do they exhibit a labored takeoff with legs dangling. C aloft, however, they are capable of long distance flights between islands. They are omnivores, takin(sects as well as plant parts and seeds. Nesting has not been studied at Palau, but elsewhere the ne built on the water, anchored to emergent plants. Clutches may be large, and the black downy chicks swim immediately. Bottom, right: adult and juvenile photographed with Yellow Bittern at Ngardok Lake

as Dove

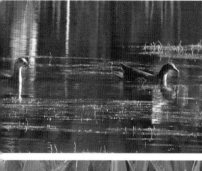

PURPLE SWAMPHEN/ UEK
Porphyrio porphyrio pelewensis   Rallid

L 43 cm, 17 in. The Purple Swamphen has an amazingly broad but patchy distribution from south
Europe and South Africa through the Asian tropics to the Indo-Pacific as far as Samoa. Palau has its o
endemic subspecies, one of about a dozen and the only one in Micronesia. It is known from Babelda
Koror, Peleliu and Angaur. It is one of the largest wild birds in Palau, and a stunning one to look at. It is o
purplish blue, more purple on the back, with a huge red bill that extends back over the forehead as a shi
red legs, and bright white undertail coverts prominent in aggressive displays. The Palau bird's dark co
ing makes it one of the more distinctive subspecies. Despite their almost gaudy colors, Purple Swamph
are not easy to observe (or photograph) because they are very shy, and run for cover at the least dis
bance. They have a wide variety of vocalizations, often heard at night. The most common call is a h
clear *skeek*, but many other squawks, cackles, whistles, and screeches are heard, especially when
birds are agitated. Note the small chick hiding behind the adults in the photo below.

Despite its status as a unique subspecies, and its declining numbers, the Purple Swamphen is one of o
two endemic birds not protected by law in Palau. This came about because swamphens are believed to
destructive to taro fields, and they do, indeed, eat taro. Traditionally, however, local "taro ladies" did
persecute or kill Swamphens because they believed that doing so would result in a bad crop, or destruc
of the crop by the dead bird's angry kin. Instead, they would talk to the bird, giving it permission to eat t
taro, but ask it to leave some for them. In recent years, however, taro crops have been tended to by h
immigrant workers who know nothing of this traditional protection provided for the swamphens, and t
often kill the birds when they can. Taro farm owners MTE interviewed remarked on the declining numb
of **uek**, especially on Koror. It would be a shame if one of Palau's endemics, especially such a spectac
one, would go extinct for lack of protection.

Despite persecution, Purple Swamphens remain widespread on Babeldaob, albeit in reduced numbe
Their existence at Palau appears to be completely tied to taro farming, because they are almost ne
seen far from an active or abandoned taro patch. Taro farmers say that Purple swamphens prefer the s
high quality species of taro root, just like Palauans do, but perhaps a switch to growing more other typ
would allow the birds to survive without competing with humans for food.They are also attracted to I
nanas growing near taro fields, and eat young banana shoots as well as the fruit, obtained by climbing
into the trees. In other parts of the world, swamphens eat a variety of aquatic plants that have soft roots
tubers, but Palau has few such plants and taro is just too easy for the birds to find, which creates a probl
for the local farmers.

Purple Swamphens have several displays that involve bowing, posturing and flashing the white under
feathers. When displaying, they may stand uncharacteristically in full view. Flicking of the tail to show
the white feathers is not used to attract mates, but is an aggressive display directed at predators (such
humans, which are predators to them). It indicates that the bird is alert to the threat and pursuit would
futile (see below left, and previous page). Bowing displays without showing the white undertail are usec
courtship. Purple Swamphens are strongly territorial, driving all rivals away, but a territory may be occup
by several apparent adults because young from previous years may remain as helpers. The bulky nes
made of aquatic plants and anchored in dense vegetation in shallow water, but usually not actually float.
Both sexes and the helpers participate in building, although the male mostly brings the materials for
female to place in the nest. Clutch size at Palau is not known, but elsewhere is 2-7 eggs. The eggs are p
brown or cream spotted with brown and purple. Like those of other rails, the black chicks are precocial a
nidifugous, and may leave the nest as soon as they hatch if there is a threat, or be brooded in the nest
a while. They are cared for by their parents for up to two months before fledging.

H Douglas Pratt

H Douglas Pratt

WHITE-BROWED CRAKE
SNGORECH
Poliolimnas cinereus   Ralli

L 18 cm, 7 in. Palau's smallest rail is a very secre
inhabitant of freshwater ponds, marshy places,
patches, and occasionally brackish ponds. It is the m
difficult of all resident birds to see at Palau. On othe
lands such as Yap, where these photos were taken
easier to see, though still shy. The upperparts
olive-brown, with darker centers to the feathers that
duce some faint streaking. The throat is gray, w
gradually shades to buff on the belly and undertai
verts. It has a boldly marked face, with white st
above and below the eye. The yellow bill, with a tin
red at the base, is short and chickenlike. The eyes
eyelids are blood red. These crakes are found
southeastern Asia and the Philippines to northern
tralia, Fiji, and Samoa, including the high islands o
cronesia from Palau east to Pohnpei, although it is
extirpated from Guam. They have been seen rec
on Babeldaob (Lake Ngardok) and Peleliu, and
known from Koror and Angaur, but absent from
Rock Islands. Members of a pair call back and
while foraging with a high-pitched *squeak-it* and a
gutteral *geck-oh*. When excited, they may produce
licking chorus of *hee* notes, almost as if they are la
ing because we can't see them! They forage,
wading, along the water's edge and their long
enable them to walk on large leaves such as taro.

PACIFIC BLACK DUCK
DEBAR
Anas superciliosa pelewensis   Ana

L 55 cm, 22 in. Whether Palau's only breeding duc
survives is uncertain. Formerly called the Gray Du
is a relative of the domestic Mallard, and females
the familiar *quack*. It is dark brownish gray on the
with paler sides of the head. The face is marked b
prominent dark streaks, one through the eye, the
from the base of the bill across the lower cheek. Th
is gray, and the feet are orange or yellow. In fligh
wing shows a flash of metallic green in the seconda
The species is found from Indonesia through Aus
and on islands as far east as Tahiti. The island po
tions all belong to a single subspecies, named for
where it was first described for science. It is dec
through its range, and the Palau population is o
verge of extirpation, if not already gone. Originally
on Babeldaob, Koror, Peleliu and Angaur, the
recent reports were from Lake Ngardok and po
Angaur, but it is easily confused with migratory duc

MIGRATORY DUCKS

veral species of ducks *Anatidae* migrate to Palau
n time to time. They are never present in large
nbers, and not all species are found every year,
most ducks seen at Palau today are migrants
n Eurasia. These ducks are almost never seen
salt water, and are confined to the relatively few
hwater ponds, lakes, and reservoirs. They are
ally very shy and difficult to approach, and fly at
least disturbance. They are, after all, used to
ng shot at, even in Palau. Ducks have an unusual
ern of molts and plumages, wherein, after nest-
the drake (male) molts into a so-called eclipse
nage that resembles that of the much duller hen.
s plumage is worn for only a short time, but many
kes are still wearing their dull body plumage
en they arrive in Palau. The drakes gradually
ume their bright breeding plumage over the next
months, and complete it well before they fly back
th. Many ducks have a metallic or contrasting
ch of color across the secondaries called a
culum. Migratory ducks usually show up in Octo-
and November, and depart by the end of March.

)RTHERN PINTAIL   W
as acuta   Anatidae

cm, 26 in. (tail not included) Probably the most
nerous of the ducks to visit Palau in the northern
ter, the Northern Pintail is quite distinctive. It has
aceful, long-necked profile and both sexes have
ng-pointed tail, which in the male may be quite
ended. The pointed tail is most evident in flight. In
eding plumage, the male has a brown head and
e foreneck that extends into the brown behind
eye. Northern Pintails are found all around the
hern hemisphere. MTE saw 14 birds in 2007, in
aur, Peleliu, Lake Ngardok, the Ngatpang aqua-
ure ponds, and Koror.

Eclipse Drake
185

Drake
Thomas Dove

Hen

186

Drake

Martin Hale

Hen

TUFTED DUCK
Aythya fuligula   Ana

L 43 cm, 17 in. Tufted Ducks are fairly frequen
tors to Palau, but in very low numbers. A fe
probably present every year, especially on A
They are not colorful, hens and eclipse drakes
mostly plain dark brown with gray bills. In fligh
show a bold white bar across the secondarie
tending into the primaries. Breeding males are
handsome, black with white flanks, with a pror
tuft that hangs off the back of the head, but the
rarely seen at Palau. Females may show a sh
as well. In 2007 these ducks were seen at A
Peleliu, Ngardok Lake, and the Ngatpang aq
ture ponds. Different species of migratory duc
iting Palau often hang out together, as the
Duck below, seen here feeding together v
Northern Pintail hen on Angaur.

EURASIAN WIGEON V
Anas penelope Anatidae

. 51 cm, 20 in. This handsome duck is only a rare
visitor to Palau, and should not be expected yearly.
The male has a gray body and rusty-red head with a
cream-colored crown and forehead. Females are
rusty brown. Males have a large white patch on the
forewing that helps distinguish eclipse drakes from
females. Both sexes show the characteristic pale
blue bill with black tip.

187

Thomas Dove

EURASIAN TEAL W
Anas crecca Anatidae

37 cm, 14.5 in. Teal are small ducks, and this is the
smallest one to visit Palau. Both sexes have a metallic green speculum. Females are otherwise just
mottled brown ducks with a faint pattern of stripes on
the side of the head, but males have a gray body and
reddish brown head, with a streak of metallic green
that surrounds the eye and sweeps backward from it
toward the nape. The male's bill is gray, but the
female's has an orange tinge along the edge.

GARGANEY W
Anas querquedula Anatidae

39 cm, 15.5 in. The Garganey is a teal found
mostly in Eurasia and Africa, but it wanders widely. It
is an uncommon visitor to Palau. Hens and eclipse
drakes are difficult to distinguish from Eurasian Teal,
but note their lack of green in the secondaries and
stronger face pattern, which usually shows a round
white spot at the base of the bill below the eye stripe.
Gray and brown breeding drakes are very distinctive
with a bold white streak above the eye that sweeps
back and curves down toward the nape, obvious
pale gray forewings, and dark speculum bordered
fore and aft with white.

H Douglas Pratt

Jacob Faust

SHOREBIRDS

Shorebirds, also known as waders, form a special category of the avian world that includes a cluster of bird families adapted to life on the ground and in shallow water, and shorelines, whether fresh or salt, provide both. They share a common ancestry with gulls and terns, but are very different from them in appearance, ecology, and behavior. All shorebirds feed exclusively on small animals of various kinds, and they have subdivided this ecological niche by developing a variety of bill shapes and lengths and many different feeding techniques. Of the 12 shorebird families known worldwide (some of them very small with localized distribution), only 4 are found in Palau, but these represent the largest and most widespread ones. They are characterized as follows:

Plovers Charadriidae are plump, compact shorebirds with short bills. They have relatively short necks and legs, and feed with a run-and-pick or run-and-stab method. They are more likely than most other shorebirds to have bold color patterns, although some are more intricately mottled or streaked. They are also more likely to be seen in upland settings away from shores or mudflats than other shorebirds.

Stilts Recurvirostridae are long-legged and long-necked wading birds with bold black, white, and reddish brown color patterns. Stilts are black-and-white, with pink legs and long needlelike bills. The family also includes the avocets, which have not yet been found in Palau, that have long upturned bills.

Sandpipers and snipes Scolopacidae, the largest shorebird family, includes such a wide variety of birds that they are given many different subgroup names. Nearly all of them have mottled, streaked, or spotted plumage. They feed by probing in the sand or mud, or picking continuously at the surface, with the head held down for long periods. They do not run and stab like plovers. The namesake typical sandpipers are usually small, with upright posture, long necks and legs, and bills of varying length, some quite long. Some of the larger sandpipers are named for the color of their legs (greenshank, redshank, yellowlegs) and are collectively called "shanks". Others have distinctive individual or 2-species names (**Sanderling**, Dunlin, knots, tattlers, turnstones). The largest members of this family fall into two groups, the **curlews** with downcurved bills, and the **godwits** with straight or upturned bills. The smallest sandpipers are collectively called "peeps" and include the birds best known in the eastern hemisphere as **stints**. These tiny shorebirds form flocks that wheel about in tight formations. Finally, the **snipes**, with plump, compact bodies and long bills for probing in mud, are cryptically colored birds of marshes and swamps.

Pratincoles Glareolidae are rather odd short-legged shorebirds that are much more aerial than others, with long narrow wings and buoyant, tern-like flight.

Shorebirds are highly migratory, and none of them breed in Palau. Many species are cosmopolitan in distribution, breeding around the high arctic, and wintering into the southern hemisphere. The Sanderling, for example, appears on the species list for every continent and major island group. Many different species winter on tropical Pacific islands such as Palau, or pass through on migration in spring and fall. All adult shorebirds have two plumages. The basic or nonbreeding plumage is worn for most of the time the birds are on their wintering grounds, and is usually not colorful. From March onward, shorebirds begin to acquire their alternate or breeding plumage, which can be spectacularly colorful. In the fall, many of the shorebirds seen in Palau are juveniles hatched in the same year. They can be recognized by plumages that are like adult basic, but often more richly colored.

PACIFIC GOLDEN PLOVER/ DERARIIK
Pluvialis fulva

W

Charadriida

L 27 cm, 10.5 in. The Pacific Golden Plover is one of Palau's most familiar shorebirds. It can be seen open habitats everywhere in the islands, but especially along roadsides, on grassy lawns, on tidal mud flats, and even in villages. This species nests on the arctic tundra of Siberia and western Alaska, bu spends most of its year in the Indo-Pacific region and Australasia, as well as the islands of Oceania. few nonbreeding individuals may even spend the summer months in Palau, but they are mainly presen from late August to May. During that time, they mostly wear their rather drab yellow-brown basic plum age, plain below and mottled and spangled with gold and dark brown above. Just before they fly north however, they take on their spectacular breeding (or alternate) plumage with black underparts, a bol white stripe along the flanks, and bold gold and white spots above. In the fall, juvenile birds of the yea can be told from adults by their stronger golden tinge throughout the plumage.

Pacific Golden Plovers exhibit the "run-and-stab" feeding method typical of plovers in general. It is on way plovers can be told at a distance from other shorebirds such as sandpipers and stints, that tend pick and probe. Golden plovers eat nearly any kind of small animal they can catch, from crabs to insect Many individuals maintain feeding territories where the same bird can be seen day after day. At nigh however, they leave their territories and gather in large flocks in safer places to roost. Such places i clude runways or other very open places where approaching predators could easily be spotted, or eve rooftops. When roosting flocks gather, they make a lot of noise with their whistled calls. Such choruse are different from the typical alarm call, a loud *chew-weeep!* given by birds startled into flight.

Palau also hosts several other species of plover, discussed on the following pages, that also breed in th arctic and winter in the tropics. None of them are as common as the Pacific Golden, but small numbe are present every year. The Gray Plover is slightly larger, but all others are smaller and generally pla brown above, white below, with a band across the breast that is either complete or broken in the midc

Eric VanderWerf

GRAY PLOVER
Pluvialis squatarola   Charadrii

L 29 cm, 11.5 in. This uncommon visitor to Pa resembles the Pacific Golden Plover in size color pattern, but it is never as golden on the b In flight, it is easily distinguished by its white ru bold white wing stripe, and black patches ur the wings. In breeding plumage, it has black derparts, and a black-and-white pattern on back. Americans know it as the Black-be Plover. It breeds in the circumpolar arctic.

Thomas Dove

COMMON RINGED PLOVER
Charadrius hiaticula   Charadrii

L 15 cm, 6 in. This smaller plover is uncommc Palau where it is usually seen feeding in c tidal flats. Its bright orange legs distinguish it the similar, and more common, Little ringed pl (below), as does the bold white wing stripe vis in flight. The call is a quiet, flute-like *tooe* breeding plumage, the Common Ringed Pl shows a face and breast band pattern simila that of Little Ringed, but with a bright orange l to the bill and no white behind the black ban the forehead. It breeds in the high arctic and ters mostly in southern Europe and Africa, wanderers visit Palau.

The similar **Kentish Plover** *C. alexandrinus* shown) also visits Palau. It has black leg broken breast band, and paler crown.

LRP breeding

Michelle & Peter Wong

LITTLE RINGED PLOVER
Charadrius dubius   Charadrii

LRP nonbreeding

L 15 cm, 6 in. This species nests across ce Eurasia and winters in the old world tropics in ing Palau, where it is the most common s plover. It is more likely to turn up at inland such as aquaculture ponds than the other plo Compared to the C.Ringed, it lacks the bold wing stripe and has yellowish or dull pink, ra than orange, legs and a narrow but prom yellow eyering. The bill is black, with no oran the base. The call is a quiet downslurred wh Breeding plumage is strongly marked with a l breast band, black ear patch, and black across the forehead bordered on both side white.

...ESSER SAND PLOVER M

...aradrius mongolus   Charadriidae

...9 cm, 7.5 in. The two sand plovers are uncom-
...n at Palau. They are larger, with longer legs,
... more likely to be seen on sandy beaches. A
...aller, more delicate bill and shorter, dark legs
...inguish this smaller species, formerly called
...ngolian Plover. In breeding plumage the ear
...ch becomes black and the breast takes on a
...utiful rusty-orange tone. Those seen in April
... May will be transitioning to colorful plumage
...ore returning to their breeding grounds scat-
...d across eastern Siberia and western China.

...REATER SAND PLOVER M

...aradrius leschenaultii   Charadriidae

...3 cm, 9 in. This larger sand plover is most
...ly distinguished by its relatively much larger
...It also usually has paler legs. Calls of the two
...cies are similar enough that they are not much
... in telling them apart. Like its smaller relative,
... plover takes on a striking breeding plumage
...re it migrates north in the spring, but the
...y-orange does not spread so far down the
...s. This species breeds inland across the
...pes of central Asia, and winters on southern
...es from Africa to Australia, including Palau.

Thomas Dove

...ACK-WINGED STILT W

...antopus himantopus   Recurvirostridae

...3 am, 15 in. Stilts characteristically wade in
...low waters where they feed on insects and
...atic animals. The only species to visit Palau is
...kely to be mistaken for any other bird here,
... its bright pink legs, bold black-and-white
...nage, and long straight bill. Females are
...wner on the back than males. Individuals of
... sexes vary in the amount of dark gray
...dging they show on the back of the head and
...k, and some have none. Black-winged Stilts
...d across central Eurasia and winter from
...heast Asia and the Philippines to Australia.
...y year, a few individuals turn up in Palau.
...ugh rare, they seem to be increasing in num-
... in recent years. Look for them around aqua-
...re and sewage ponds and shallow lagoons
... Babeldaob to Peleliu.

GRAY-TAILED TATTLER
Heteroscelus brevipes   Scolopaci

L 25 cm, 10 in. Tattlers are medium-sized plain gray sandpipers with a rather elongated profile, long and dull yellow legs. The leg color helps distinguish them from other shorebirds in Palau with which might be confused. There are two species of tattler, but this one is by far the most common in Palau, wh it is probably the most common sandpiper. Both species are plain gray above, white below, with a white eyebrow and dark lores. In the most often seen nonbreeding plumage, they are very difficult to apart (both have gray tails). This species is always a little paler and subtly browner than the Wandering tler (next page), but lighting can erase those differences. The eyebrows of the Gray-tailed Tattler are mally broader, and usually meet above the bill. The best key is the voice, but that varies in both spec Gray-tailed Tattlers characteristically utter a 2-noted alarm call *too-weet!* like a quiet version of the Pa Golden Plover call, but they also sometimes give a trill like that of a Wandering tattler. In breeding pl age, the Gray-tailed are more finely barred below, which never reaches the undertail coverts.

Gray-tailed Tattlers in Palau prefer open tidal with mangrove borders, but at high tide often gregate on concrete docks or rock jetties. W feeding, they bob and teeter like Common Sa pipers, picking constantly at rocks for small cr probing in sand for worms, or catching small fis shallow pools. Very rarely, they may be found a rocky inland streams, or even perched in tr They breed in eastern Siberia (it was also calle berian Tattler before), and winters along shore Malaysia and the Philippines to Australia.

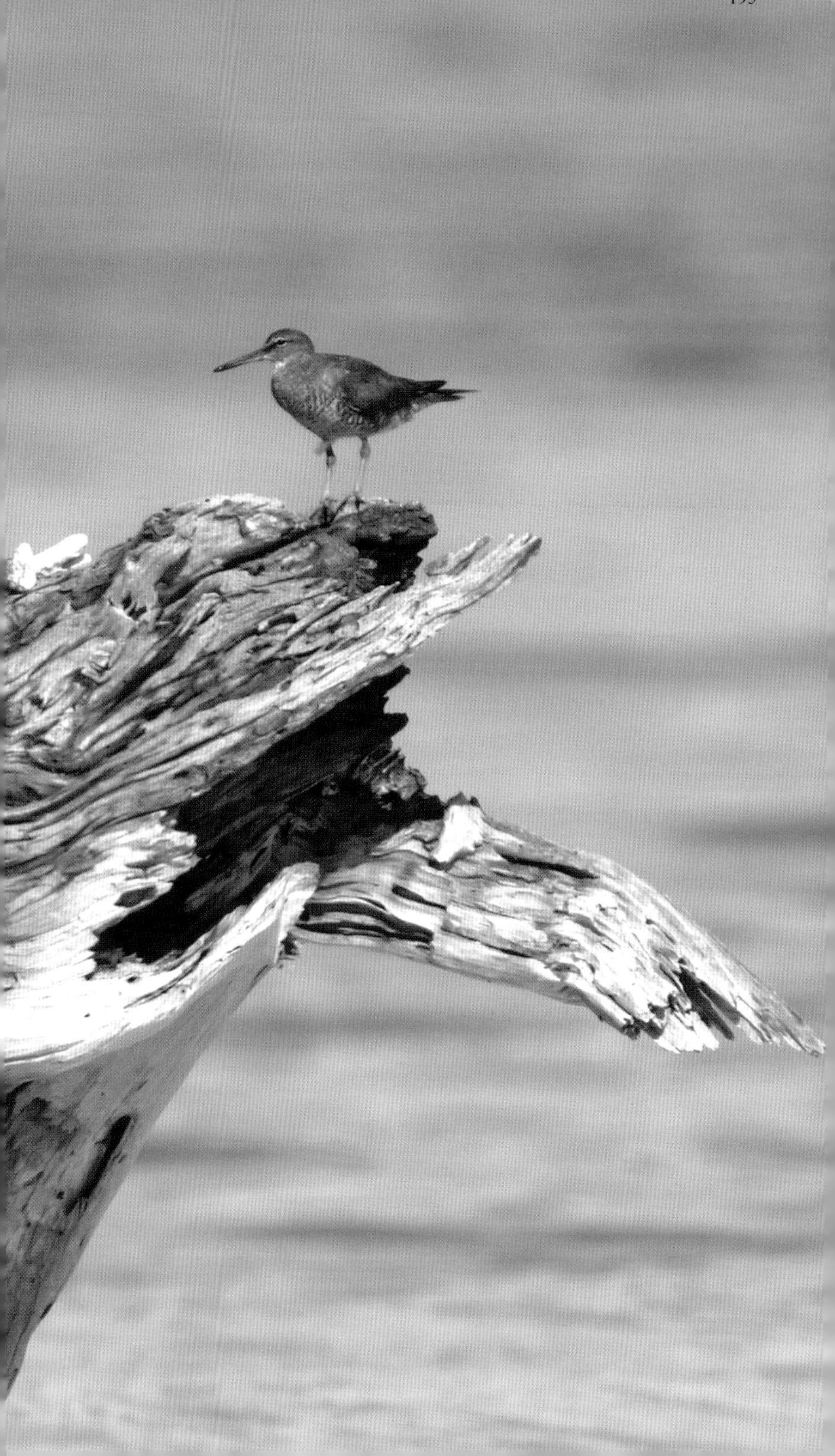

Thomas Dove

H Douglas Pratt

WANDERING TATTLER

Heteroscelus incanus Scolopacidae

L 25 cm, 10 in. The "other" tattler at Palau, th Wandering is far less common than the Gray tailed. It breeds in Alaska and western Canad and winters along continental coasts and on lands across the tropical Pacific. Palau is near th western extreme of its distribution. It is darker a more blue-gray above, and its eyebrows do n meet above the bill. Its flight call is a ringing quavering trill *too-li-li-li-li-li* but it can utter 2 syllable calls somewhat like those of Gray-tail Tattlers. The breeding plumage (lower phot shows bold barring on the underparts, includi the undertail coverts, and is acquired earlier th in the Gray-tailed Tattler, so is more often seen the tropics.

RUDDY TURNSTONE

Arenaria interpres Scolopacidae

L 24 cm, 9.5 in. Turnstones are stocky shorebir shaped more like plovers than sandpipers. Th have odd, slightly upturned triangular bills, w which they overturn rocks, shells, or other flotsa washed up on the shore as they search for pr items. The Ruddy Turnstone is a cosmopolit species that breeds in the circumpolar high arct and winters on all continents and islands to t south. It is a common visitor to Palau from Augu to May, and a few nonbreeders may occasiona stay year round. Turnstones often associate w Pacific Golden Plovers in upland grassy habit or in flat areas such as runways and docks.

In all plumages, Ruddy Turnstones have bri orange legs. In flight (facing page) they show striking and unmistakable black-and-white patte with a broad white wing stripe connecting to white rump, a black tail tip, a secondary str along the outer edge of the scapulars, and a wh slash up the middle of the back. In nonbreed plumage (top, left) the rest of the upperparts dull dark brown, the underparts white with smud round dark patches on the sides of the breast March, turnstones begin to acquire their beaut breeding plumage (bottom, left) in which much the brown is replaced by bright rusty-orange a the head and breast develop an intricate blac and-white harlequin pattern.

Eric VanderWerf

COMMON SANDPIPER W
BENGOBAINGUKL
Actitis hypoleucos   Scolopacida

L 20 cm, 8 in. This sandpiper is a familiar bird
Palau, mostly from August to May, but with a fe
present all year. It frequents shorelines and tid
flats, and can be seen inland along gravel roa
sides or feeding along streams and in rain pool
It is recognized by its distinctive flight, with alte
nating quick flaps and long glides on stifly bowec
down wings. It shows a bold white wing stripe ar
tail margins. As it takes off, the bird usually give
a high-pitched ringing 3-note whistle *twee-wee
weet*. Common Sandpipers have a characteris
bobbing or teetering motion as they walk. The
wade in shallow water or walk methodically alor
the edge, searching for any kind of animal pre
They may perch on emergent posts or snag
overhanging tree branches, or man-made objec
such as boats. Adult Common Sandpipers a
plain khaki above, clear white below, with the da
extending as a smudge onto the sides of th
breast, and a pale eyebrow. Fall juveniles ha
orange-buff edges and dark subterminal bands o
the dorsal feathers, especially on the shoulde
and wing coverts. Adults show this pattern only o
the shoulder. They breed across temperate Eu
asia, and winter from Africa to Australia.

Thomas Dove

WOOD SANDPIPER W

Tringa glareola Scolopacidae

20 cm, 8 in. Seen throughout Palau, this is the most common passage-migrant shorebird in Palau. Small flocks appear in August-November and March-May, when this becomes the "default sandpiper" here. One can assume all medium-sized gray sandpipers are Woodies unless proven otherwise. Larger than stints, but smaller than the "shanks", they have a preference for muddy habitats, such as the edges of taro patches or sewage and aquaculture ponds.

In their southbound migration, adult Wood Sandpipers are dark brownish gray above, spangled with small buff and white spots, and white below with the sides of the neck and breast washed or mottled with gray. Juveniles are more heavily spotted and tinged with buff on the breast. Northbound birds may show the breeding plumage, which is more heavily spotted and edged above and has distinct streaks on the neck and breast. Always they show greenish or yellow legs, a white rump, indistinct barring on the tail, and a bold eyebrow that extends back well behind the eye. The only Palau visitor likely to cause confusion with the Wood Sandpiper is the very rare Green Sandpiper, which is darker overall in color.

The Wood Sandpiper's bill is of moderate length, a bit longer than the rest of the head. It is used to probe the mud for crustaceans and worms. The birds may teeter a bit, but not so noticeably as the Common Sandpiper. When startled, Woodies take to the air with very erratic and acrobatic flight, and may utter their 3-note *jif-jif-jif* call, lower pitched and less piercing than that of the Common Sandpiper. Wood Sandpipers breed in the boreal zone across northern Eurasia, and winter in Africa, and from India to Australia.

GREEN SANDPIPER V

Tringa ochropus Charadriidae

20 cm, 8 in. This species is very rare in Palau, and only recently confirmed by MTE's photos. Green Sandpipers look very much like Wood Sandpipers, but are darker above, with fewer spots, and have dark wing linings (right, bottom). The eyebrow extends back to a bold eyering, but not much behind the eye, and the tail has 2 bold horizontal bars, barely visible in this photo. The range is similar to that of the Wood Sandpiper, but they do not winter as far south. Photo was taken at the Malakal sewage ponds.

RUFF
Philomachus pugnax   Charadriic

L 31 cm, 12 in. Female 25 cm, 10 in. This sandpi
is highly variable in individual plumage and b
size, with females, called reeves, being m
smaller. Nonbreeding birds are colored like the
cific Golden Plover, but have a more upright post
and long pointed bill. Their legs vary from gray to
pink to orange, but are never dark. The face
always pale, especially at the base of the bill.
bird gets its name from the neck frills that breec
males exhibit. They nest across n. Eurasia, winte
in widely scattered spots from Europe to Australi

LONG-TOED STINT
Calidris subminutus   Charadriic

L 15 cm, 6 in. The stints are the smallest shoreb
in Palau. The Long-toed is identified by its stra
yellow legs. Nonbreeding birds are brownish-g
on the back, but spring birds are redder, looking
small Sharp-tailed Sandpipers. They are late sp
migrants, passing through muddy freshwater site
Palau when many other shorebirds have already
parted. They nest in boreal Siberia and winter f
India to Australia.

RED-NECKED STINT
Calidris ruficollis   Charadriic

L 15 cm, 6 in. Named for its rusty red bree
colors, the Red-necked Stint is usually seen at Pा
in its plain gray-and-white basic plumage. Black
help distinguish it from the Long-toed Stint. M
spend their winters in Palau, feeding in small to la
flocks on tidal flats, runways and grassy lawns. T
nest in the high arctic of e.Siberia and winter
se. Asia to New Zealand.

H. Douglas Pratt

SANDERLING
Calidris alba   Charadrii

L 20 cm, 8 in. Larger and paler than the stints,
Sanderling frequents sandy shores and flats. I
breeding adults are nearly white with a black sh
der. Juveniles have black markings on the b
Breeding plumage is rusty red on the head
neck. The Sanderling is the only small shorebi
lack a hind toe. It nests in the high arctic and wir
to the s. hemisphere worldwide. Uncommoɪ
Palau.

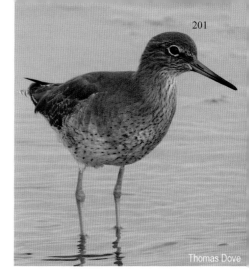

OMMON REDSHANK M

nga totanus   Charadriidae

8 cm, 11 in. The Redshank is well named be-
use its legs, and also the base of its straight bill
bright orange-red, making this an easy shore-
ds to identify. It is a mostly dull brown bird oth-
vise, showing more streaking in the spring than
he fall. In flight, it shows a bold triangle of white
he trailing edge of the wings and a white blaze
the middle of the back. It is an uncommon pas-
e migrant in Palau, where it favors tidal flats,
ddy wetlands, and wet grassy fields. It nests in
temperate zone across Eurasia, and winters
ng coasts from Europe to the Philippines.

Thomas Dove

ECTORAL SANDPIPER M

lidris melanotos   Charadriidae

2 cm, 8.5 in. The Pectoral is a streaked buffy
wn bird with straw-yellow legs that varies in
e (males are larger than females). It is easily
ntified by the sharp demarcation between the
aked breast and plain belly. It is an uncommon
sage migrant at Palau, likely to be confused
y with the Sharp-tailed Sandpiper (below) with
ch it often associates. It breeds in the high
tic of eastern Siberia and N.America, and win-
s in southern Australia, New Zealand, and S.
erica.

Thomas Dove

HARP-TAILED SANDPIPER

lidris acuminata   Charadriidae M

2 cm, 8.5 in. The Sharp-tailed Sandpiper lacks
sharp demarcation between the streaked
ast and plain belly that the Pectoral Sandpiper
. It often shows a reddish cap and honey-
red tinge to the breast. It is also uncommon at
au, and breeds in the high arctic of eastern Si-
a, wintering throughout Australasia.

Thomas Dove

URLEW SANDPIPER M

ldris ferruginea   Charadriidae

cm, 8.5 in. Named for its curlew-like bill, this
n uncommon migrant in Palau that breeds in
northern Siberia and winters from Africa to
tralia. It is plain gray with white below, and a
eyebrow. The similar but very rare **Dunlin** C.
a (not shown) has a less curved bill, no white
o, and shorter legs.

Thomas Dove

MARSH SANDPIPER
Tringa stagnatilis   Charadriid

L 25 cm, 10 in. This long-legged sandpiper loo
like a miniature Greenshank (photo of both bir
below), but is much smaller and more delicate, w
a very thin, needle-like bill, and darker legs in no
breeding plumage (gray above, white belo
Breeding birds are browner, mottled above, w
bold spots on the neck and breast. It breeds in
Asian steppes and winters from Africa to Austral

COMMON GREENSHANK
Tringa nebularia   Charadriid

L 34 cm, 13.5 in. This is a large shorebird wit
long, slightly upturned bill. It is mostly gray w
white underparts and greenish-gray legs. Bef
leaving in the spring, it may show streaks on
foreneck and breast. It is uncommon at Palau,
conspicuous because of its large size. It feeds
shallow water of tidal flats, muddy shores of fre
water ponds, and even in garbage dumps. It wa
steadily, stabbing at prey it disturbs. It is a shy a
solitary bird that flies away when startled givin
loud *cheew* call. It breeds in the boreal zone fr
Britain to Kamchatka, and winters from s. Europe
s. Africa and New Zealand.

EREK SANDPIPER M

enus cinereus Charadriidae

23 cm, 9 in. This is the only small shorebird with
strongly upturned bill. Its short yellow-orange
gs give it a low-slung profile like that of tattlers,
th which it often associates. They are a plain
ownish-gray above and white below, with a pale
ebrow. Breeding plumage differs in having a
ack horizontal line in the scapulars over the
ng. Juveniles are browner, with buff edges to
e dorsal feathers. Tereks bob and teeter like
ommon Sandpipers, and are very active feed-
s, favoring tidal flats. They breed across n. Eur-
ia and winter from Africa to Australia, passing
rough Palau on both legs of the journey.

WINHOE'S SNIPE W

allinago megala Charadriidae

27 cm, 10.5 in. Snipes are compact, cryptically
lored brown birds that feed by probing their long
s in the mud of their marshy or swampy habi-
s. They are hard to see on the ground, and
en fly away before you realize they are there.
hen startled into flight, they often give a loud
spy *zhrick* like the sound of tearing cloth. There
e several species of snipe that all look much
ke, but this is the only one officially recorded
m Palau. Swinhoe's shows no white trailing
ge to the secondaries in flight, unlike the
mmon Snipe *G.gallinago*, which has been re-
rded from as close as Yap. Swinhoe's Snipe is
uncommon winter resident of Palau, and
eds in north-central Asia, wintering from India
w. Micronesia and New Guinea. It arrives in
tober-November, and leaves by March.

RIENTAL PRATINCOLE V

areola maldivarum Glareolidae

5 cm, 10 in. This unusual shorebird is more like
ern than a sandpiper. It is a strong flier with its
g, narrow, swept-back wings, and feeds
allow-like on flying insects. On the ground, it
sents a long thin profile. It is a handsome bird
n a pale buffy throat, black collar and red-
sed black bill. In flight, it displays a white rump
a slightly forked short black tail. They breed in
and se. Asia, migrate to New Guinea and n.
stralia, and are irregular visitors to Palau.

Dan Vice

WHIMBREL/ OKAK
Numenius phaeopus

W

Charadriida

L 45 cm, 17.5 in. The Whimbrel is the most common curlew, indeed the most common large shorebir in Palau, and a good point of reference for identifying the less common species. It is intermediate in siz and easily distinguished by a combination of bold dark stripes on the head and a white slash in th middle of the back, visible in flight. The white patch is variable, and may show some dark barring. Th subspecies that visits Palau breeds in far eastern Siberia and winters south to Australia and New Zea land. Most of them arrive in September-October, and depart in April-May, but a few individuals can b found year round. In Palau, Whimbrels are found in a wide variety of habitats, but especially tidal area with reefs or dredged spoil banks. They may also rest or roost in mangroves, and are the only shorebir in Palau that routinely perches in trees. Whimbrels feed by probing the sand or mud for small burrowin animals, or picking items from the surface such as crabs. They may form flocks of up to a dozen or mor birds. Their manner of flight over long distances is reminiscent of that of ducks, with rapid wingbeats. O takeoff, they often utter their whistled call tee-*tee-tee-tee-tee-tee-tee* on a level pitch. Birders in Pala should be alert for the North American subspecies of Whimbrel, which lacks the white back patch an may be a separate species **Hudsonian Curlew** *N. hudsonicus*. It is seen occasionally in Hawaii an New Zealand, and may reach Palau. Even more likely to turn up is the **Bristle-thighed Curlew** *N. tah tiensis*, which is widespread in the tropical Pacific, including eastern Micronesia with sightings as fa west as Yap, but not yet Palau. It is very similar to the Whimbrel, but with a peach-colored brown-barre rump and tail and a very different 3-note whistled call *tee-oo-weet*. The best spots to find Whimbrels Palau by car are the Ngiwal State and Ngatpang State reef flats at low tide.

Thomas D

Michelle & Peter Wong

LITTLE CURLEW
Numenius minutes   Charadrii

L 31 cm, 12 in. This small curlew (about the siz
a Pacific Golden Plover) looks like a minia
Whimbrel with a bill that is only slightly decur
It is mainly a bird of upland grassy habitats, s
as airports or the grounds of the Palau cap
where they feed by picking. Their call is a ha
chew-chew-chew. Little Curlews breed in no
central Siberia and winter in Australia and I
Guinea. A few individuals pass through Pa
each year both north- and southbound.

EASTERN CURLEW
Numenius madagascariensis   Charadrii

L 58 cm, 23 in. Much larger than the Whimbrel
Eastern Curlew has a much longer, deeply cu
bill and lacks bold stripes on the head or a w
patch on the back. Feeding, it is more of a pro
pushing its long bill deep into the mud. Its flig
more languid, and it may form small flocks. It
regular but uncommon passage migrant in Pa
Its call is a high-pitched *kerleee*. It breeds ir
Russian Far East, and winters in Australasia.

BAR-TAILED GODWIT
imosa lapponica

M

Charadriidae

41 cm, 16 in. Godwits are large mottled brown shorebirds with very long slightly upturned bills. the Bar-tailed is the more common of the 2 species that visit Palau. Some birds are grayish, others more brown. In late spring, some may show traces of the breeding plumage, which is all brick red on the head, neck and underparts. In flight, the Bar-tailed Godwit shows no bold markings in the wings, but the rump is white and the tail finely barred with black. The subspecies that visits Palau breeds from n.Siberia to w.Alaska and winters in the Indo-Australian region. Godwits feed by probing deep in the mud or soft sand, sometimes inserting the bill up to its base. The male bird below, right, was photographed by MTE at Palau in Ngiwal State in November, 2007. It turned out that this bird had been banded and leg-flagged in May 2007 at Chongming Dongtan (near Shanghai, China). The bird was probably on a direct route across the western Pacific to nonbreeding areas like western Australia. The sand flats in the back of Carp Island are also a good spot to look for these birds at low tide.

BLACK-TAILED GODWIT
imosa limosa

M

Charadriidae

42 cm, 16.5 in. The Black-tailed Godwit (below, left) is well named, because the tail is all black, set off by a broad white rump patch. It also has bold white wing stripes obvious in flight. Its bill is longer and straighter than that of the Bar-tailed. Most birds seen in Palau will be plain gray on the upperparts and head, but still show the white markings in flight. The birds that visit Palau breed in e.Asia and migrate to Indonesia, New Guinea and Australia.

Daphne Gemmill

BIRDS OF LAGOON WATERS

The crystal clear waters of Palau's lagoon, with their spectacular growth of corals, colorful reef fish, and superb visibility are famous among divers and snorkelers the world over. A single reef system surrounds the main islands (except Angaur), making the main lagoon one of the world' largest. With an abundance of safe nesting sites among the Rock Islands, Palau's lagoon waters teem with shallow-water birds. Shallow waters over a bottom of white coral sand reflec the vibrant turquoise color on the white bellies of the birds flying overhead, making them loo blue. Lagoon waters are salt, and the birds that feed there are considered seabirds. Neverthe less, many of them rarely venture out beyond the reef. The majority of bird species in th lagoon habitat belong to the gull and tern family Laridae. **Gulls** are mainly birds of temperat regions, where they scavenge the shallow waters and shorelines for whatever they can find They have heavier bills than terns, with a hooked tip. The foods they prefer are not as readil available in the tropics, and oceanic islands have no continental shelf to produce extensiv shallow inshore waters favored by gulls, so only a few species nest in the tropics. Some, how ever, visit the tropics during the northern winter, and one species makes its way to Palau fairl regularly. **Terns** on the other hand, are abundant in tropical seas. They are active predators o small fish, either diving headfirst from the air or picking their prey from the surface with the sharp-pointed blade-like bills. Some of them nest only on remote and uninhabited islands, whil others cope with humans and other predators by nesting in tall trees. Several tern species ar nonbreeding visitors to Palau. Most terns have white body plumage and some black on th head, but the two **noddies** reverse the pattern and are dark with pale caps. The lagoon bir community is rounded out by one **cormorant** Phalacrocoracidae whose family traits are de scribed in the species account, and one **tropicbird** Phaethontidae, see introduction to nex section for description. Several birds that are discussed in other sections might just as we have been placed in this one, like the night herons and reef heron, who divide their foraging be tween fresh and salt water. One additional family should be mentioned here, the **pelicans** Pele canidae. No pelicans are found regularly in Palau, but in July 1978, from 50-100 **Australia pelicans** Pelecanus conspicillatus made their way to Palau and were seen throughout the is lands for 6-8 months, a few individuals were still seen in 1985. All eventually died or flew awa This invasion was apparently the result of a drought in the birds' nesting grounds in Australia The same year, Australian Pelicans turned up in Fiji for the only record there.

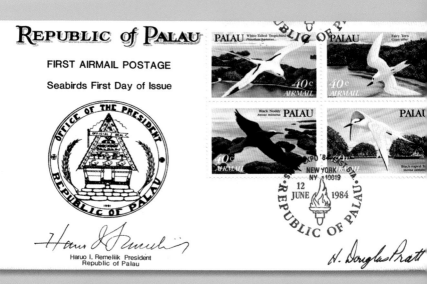

LITTLE PIED CORMORANT/ DEROECH

Phalacrocorax melanoleucos   Phalacrocoracida

L 43 cm, 17 in. Cormorants are mainly swimming birds that dive from the water surface to catch their fi
prey. They are found worldwide, but only this one species lives in Palau. Cormorants belong to a lar
and diverse order of seabirds *Pelecaniformes* that also includes pelicans, frigatebirds, tropicbirds, a
boobies. Pelicans and cormorants are more inshore birds, while members of the other families oft
feed over the open ocean (and most are discussed in the next section). Members of this order are cha
acterized by throat pouches of varying sizes and feet in which all 4 toes are webbed (the technical te
is "totipalmate"), unlike those of ducks and geese which have only the front 3 toes connected by we
bing. Cormorants have hooked bills and swim low in the water, with the bill held up at an angle rath
than parallel to the water surface. This swimming posture distinguishes them, even at a distance, fro
ducks.

Little Pied Cormorants are cleancut black and white, as if wearing a tuxedo, with bright yellow bills. Th
are found from Palau and Malaysia to Australia and New Zealand. In Palau, they are found mos
around Peleliu and Babeldaob, but can be seen anywhere. They favor coastal mangroves, freshwat
ponds and reservoirs, and occasionally marine lakes. They have a tendency to gather in small flocks, b
solitary individuals can also be found. During a dive, they can remain underwater for up to 30 second
After a period of feeding, they dry their wings by perching on trees, pilings, rocks, or buoys and holdi
the wings open. On takeoff from the water, they are slow to become airborne, running and pattering th
feet on the water, but once in the air they are strong fliers with the neck outstretched. Little Pied Corm
rants eat small fish, crustaceans, and aquatic insects, and they themselves are occasionally eaten
crocodiles. They build a platform nest of sticks in a low tree, and usually form colonies. The eggs a
plain bluish white. Their breeding biology in Palau has not been studied yet.

Immature

Juv

WHITE-TAILED TROPICBIRD/ DUDEK

Phaethon lepturus   Phaethontida

L 76 cm, 30 in. (tail is half of total). tropicbirds are well named because they are common throughout th
world's tropical seas, and only rarely wander to temperate waters. Three species make up the fami
and two of them breed in Palau. The White-tailed Tropicbird is the most familiar because the Red-tail
(next section) is found only around the most remote islands where few people live. The White-tailed
is one of the most characteristic birds of the tropical Pacific, and many consider it to be one of the worl
most beautiful birds. Even non-birders notice it because of its two extremely long central tail feathers.
plumage is mostly white, with a remarkable pearly or satin quality, and at certain seasons the breast m
take on a faint tinge of pink. The long tail streamers, despite the name, can sometimes have a peac
colored tint. The upper sides of the wings are marked by diagonal black bars across the secondary c
verts, and the outer primaries exhibit an elongated black patch. A black streak extends back from th
eye, and the bill varies from apple green to golden yellow. The black markings help distinguish th
White-tailed from the Red-tailed Tropicbird at a distance or when the birds are missing their tail strea
ers.

Tropicbirds seem to enjoy flying, spending hours on the wing without feeding or courting. They occasio
ally land on the water during the day, but they roost on the water at night. They float buoyantly with th
long tail held up at an angle, and their lift-off from the water is light and graceful. In contrast, on land th
are awkward and clumsy. Their feet are set so far back on the body that they cannot stand up like oth
birds, and they skid along on their breasts, pushing with feet and wings and sometimes pulling with t
bill. Their landings usually are more like crash-landings, sometimes with several tumbles. Nevertheles
the White-tailed Tropicbird is often seen flying over land, although it does not feed there, but only fin
a place to nest. They are true seabirds, feeding far out in the ocean, rarely even in the lagoon.

214

They take fish, especially flying-fish, and squid, by hovering briefly then diving head-first into the water. They seem curious about boats, especially those with high rigging, and will approach to investigate.

White-tailed Tropicbirds are occasionally found in groups at favored sites that produce strong updrafts, but generally they are solitary birds. In such gatherings, they utter their harsh screeching or cackling calls, which stand in sharp contrast to their graceful and delicate appearance. Such groups also form for courtship flights in which several birds may circle high overhead calling back and forth and alternating rapid wing beats and long glides. Pairs may leave the group and descend, with the male above the female, dropping his tail to touch her. The display ends when both birds go to the nest site.

At Palau, these birds usually nest in huge forest trees, while elsewhere in the Pacific they also use cliff faces where landings are easier. The nest site can be a crotch, an enclosed cavity, in a clump of bird-nest fern *Asplenium nidus*, or just on the flat top surface of a huge limb. Sometimes the only clue that a tropicbird nest is present is the long tail streamer sticking out. Only one egg, blotched and spotted with purple, is laid. Perhaps because the crash-landings are risky for the egg, incubation shifts last for several days. Both sexes incubate and feed the chick. Palauans traditionally eat tropicbirds, which often can only be caught by taking the incubating bird from the nest. The young chicks are covered with thick white down, and are quite endearing. The bill color changes first to pink, then to yellow. The chick is fed intermittently by regurgitation, and becomes very fat, weighing more than the parents at one point. After about months, the parents stop feeding and the young bird leaves the nest after slimming down for several days. At fledging, the plumage resembles the adults, but without the long tail feathers, and with the back marked with horizontal zebra stripes. These immature birds are rarely seen at Palau once they leave the nest, because they spend the next year or so far out to sea, and only return to their nesting islands when they have their adult feathering. After the chicks fledge, the adults molt and for a time lack their namesake long tail feathers. Breeding occurs throughout the year, with no defined season.

BLACK-NAPED TERN
KERKIRS
Sterna sumatrana   La

L 31 cm, 12 in. This delicate and slender tern is
distributed in the tropical Indian and southwest F
Oceans, and is common at Palau. It is nearly all
and can be mistaken at a distance for the Fairy
differs in having a very deeply forked tail, a
black bill, and a black line that connects the
around the back of the head. The outer prima
has a narrow black outer web. The upperparts a
tually very pale gray rather than white, and the
parts become pale pink during the breeding sea
is most abundant from southern Babeldaob to F
but also lives on Helen and Kayangel. Black
Terns are true inshore seabirds at Palau, seldo
turing outside the reef or sight of land. They f
swooping down to pick small fish from the surfac
occasionally plunge-diving. Black-naped Tern
join a large feeding flock of Black Noddies. F
birds often utter a sharp *krep-krep* or *chit-c*
Nesting can be at any time of year. The brown-
eggs are laid on the ground in places inacces
predators such as high sheer cliffs or small bar
offshore islets. The one or two downy chicks are
barred and spotted with black, and are fed by bc
ents with fish and crabs.

t year found a newly hatched chick that had
ft down from its nest on a cliff to the water line
rith both parents still trying to feed it. To save it
wning in the next high tide, she put it on a
s high as she could reach, still way below
s other sibling was, but the chick was immedi-
comed and fed by the parents along with the
ick further up. Fledglings resemble their par-
have streaks on the crown, some dark mot-
he back, and a dull yellow bill. Older immature
ok just like the adults but the black nape line
lge that extends down behind the eye, some-
e the pattern of a nonbreeding White-winged

de flocks of Black-naped Terns can be seen
n branches and on the Rock Island undercuts
level. A good spot to photograph them are the
markers and the old lighthouse in the harbor
where they often join Swift Terns and Noddies
en fishing.

& Peter Wong

BRIDLED TERN
BEDEBEDECHAKL
Sterna anaethetus   L

L 38 cm, 15 in. The Bridled Tern is widespread
tropical Atlantic and Indian Oceans, but is repla
most of the tropical Pacific by the closely relate
very similar Spectacled Tern *S. lunata*. Palau
Bridled's only breeding site in Micronesia, b
common here from Koror to Ngeruktabel, w
nests and roosts on high limestone cliffs, often
company of Black-naped Terns. In Palau, it is l
be confused only with the Sooty Tern, which is
seen around the main islands. The Bridled Tern
dark above and white below, but it is browner
wings and back, the black cap is separated fr
back by a narrow white collar, and the white fo
is V-shaped rather than triangular. Juveniles
white mottling above, and subadults (upper le
have a completely white face. Bridled Terns are
plunge-divers, but they tend to hunt in deepe
outside the reef, although not out of sight of lar
breeding biology of the Bridled Tern has not bee
ied at Palau. At the Cemetary Reef, a popular
spot in the Rock Island lagoon, Bridled Terns c
in close and take food thrown by people off the
catching it in midair.

BROWN NODDY/ MECHADELBEDAOCH

nous stolidus   Laridae

oddies are tropical terns named for their habit of nodding during mating displays. This is the larger of the
o species found in Palau, and it is much less common than the Black Noddy. Both species are dark brown
th pale caps as adults. The two can be difficult to tell apart, but Brown Noddies are a noticeably warmer
own color and have shorter, heavier bills and longer tails. But by far the most useful character is tail color:
arker than the back in Brown Noddy, noticeably paler than the back in Black. Juvenile or immature Brown
oddies have the pale cap reduced to a small border on the forehead.

oth noddies feed by snatching small fish from the surface of the water, but Brown Noddies tend to be soli-
ry or in small groups when feeding whereas Blacks at Palau usually hunt in large flocks. Sometimes one
2 Brown Noddies will accompany a feeding flock of Blacks. Brown Noddies are also more likely to be seen
the open ocean far away from land, where they join feeding flocks that can lead fishermen to schools of
na and other desirable fish. The larger predatory fish drive smaller ones to the surface, where they attract
abirds. The hapless small fish are then under attack from above and below! In a mixed flock, the noddies
n be identified by their different feeding habits. They do not bank and soar like shearwaters and boobies,
t flap their wings more or less constantly, and do not plunge dive like other terns, but pick their prey off the
rface. They also swim well with their webbed feet, and may rest on the water for long periods, especially
here is little wind.

own Noddies are more likely to be seen inland on high forested islands than are Black Noddies. They
metimes build their nests on horizontal limbs of big trees, and fly back and forth to the sea to feed their
ung. Their low growling calls are a familiar part of the forest bird chorus at Palau, and are often heard at
ght. On low atolls and coral islands, they may lay their eggs in just a depression in the sand. Brown Nod-
es are found throughout the world's tropics, and on all islands at Palau except Helen.

BLACK NODDY/ BEDAOCH
Anous minutus   Larid

Black Noddies are by far the more common of the two noddy species at Palau. They are a familiar sigh
they forage in large flocks over lagoon waters. They eat small fish, and when a flock discovers a schoc
shallow water, they create a huge commotion as they wheel about and snatch their prey from the water
face. Their calls are higher pitched than those of the Brown Noddy, and have a rattling quality. Black N
dies are not only smaller, but also darker than Brown Noddies. The adults have a bold white cap
shades evenly into the black of the nape and back, and a contrastingly pale gray tail, which is the best
mark for distinguishing them at a distance from Brown Noddies. Juveniles lack the contrast in the tail,
their white caps are sharply separated from the darker portions of the plumage, without the shaded tra
tion. Brown Noddies never show such a sharply defined cap in any plumage.

Black Noddies are distributed throughout the tropical Pacific, and are found on all the islands of Palau
though they nest on all islands, they are particularly abundant on the Southwest Islands of Helen and F
and on Kayangel to the north. Black Noddies usually nest colonially in trees, with a single tree suppor
many nests. Colony trees are usually near the water rather than deep in the forest. Many kinds of trees
used, but mangroves, *Pisonia grandis*, and tree heliotrope *Toumefortia argentea* seem to be favored.

Black Noddy pairs usually remain together for many seasons. Both parents participate in nest builc
Nests are made mostly of sticks and large, soft leaves that droop down over the sides. The birds do
weave materials into the nest, but simply drop them on top and shape tha mass of debris with their boc
White feces accumulate on the outside of the nest increasingly during the nesting cycle, giving it a dis
tive look and helping to hold it together as the mass decays over the weeks of incubation and chick rea

Each pair lays only a single pale egg thinly blotc
and speckled with brown. Both parents incubate,
brood the chick when it hatches after a period of
over a month, an unusually long period for this
seabird. If the nest is in bright sunlight, the ad
may leave periodically to wet their breast feath
with sea water as a cooling method.

The downy chicks differ from those of most tern.
that they resemble their parents in color pattern f
the start, with a white cap and dark body. Both
ents and chicks have bright orange-red mouth
ings, perhaps related to their unusual chick fee
habits. Unlike most terns, Black Noddies do not c
whole fish or other food items in the bill. Instead,
chick inserts its bill between the adult's mandit
and receives regurgitated food directly into its thr
The chicks fledge (leave the nest) at the age
weeks or more, but their parents continue to f
them for several weeks afterward, even though
young birds begin to forage for themselves imm
ately.

SWIFT TERN/ ROALL
Sterna bergii   Larida

L 46 cm, 18 in. Formerly called the Great Crested Tern, this species is the largest tern at Palau. It range
from the Indian Ocean through Micronesia and across the South Pacific to the Tuamotu Archipelago.
is easily distinguished by its size, large yellow bill, and shaggy crest that sticks out from the back of th
head. The upperparts are medium gray, the underparts and forehead white, and the cap black (streake
with white in nonbreeding plumage). The tail is shallowly forked, without long streamers. The voice in
cludes loud, high-pitched screams and a harsh *kriek-kriek*. The Swift Tern's flight is heavier and mor
powerful than that of smaller terns, with slower, deeper wingbeats. It is often seen perched on sandbar
pilings, channel markers, and buoys. Swift Terns catch fish in typical fashion, with spectacular headlon
dives from high overhead. Fish form almost all of their diet, although they are reported occasionally
eat other small animals such as baby sea turtles and chicks of smaller seabirds. At Palau, they forag
mostly in or near lagoon waters, but also venture out to sea a short distance.

During most of the year, Swift Terns are solitary or in small groups, but they congregate in huge numbe
for raising their young. In Palau, they nest in two colonies, a huge one on Helen Island, and smaller one
on Fana (next page) and the tiny islet of Ngeruangel (below), with the birds densely packed togethe
Wanderers from these colonies are commonly seen from Babeldaob to Peleliu, but they only nest
those three places. There are always a few Swift Terns resting together with noddies and Black-nape
Terns on the Lighthouse Channel markers around the Koror harbor entrance, and the boat channel
Carp Island dock is a favorite fishing ground where you can often see these terns teaching their youn
how to dive for fish.

The nesting season is from March to May. Each lays a single white egg, spotted with dark brown bare open sand, often very close to other eggs. downy chicks are also streaked and blotched brown. Chicks are nidifugous, that is they can le the nest soon after hatching, but they are fed by adults until they can forage on their own. Birds in nesting colony work co-operatively to protect all chicks, herding them together in a large group calle creche (pronounced *cresh*) and moving them a from threats such as people walking through colony.

A small chick, newly hatched the night before (Fana Island), will sit exposed on a beach in the burr sun waiting for the adults to come back from fishin small chicks wander too close to the water, they be attacked by crabs and voracious little moray e sometimes simultaneously! MTE captured the s on the following page of such an eel attack on a chick at Ngeruangel. The aggressive *Gymnoth* eels there are so used to hunting chicks that th even come out of the water and nip at people's when you walk close to the water's edge.

FAIRY TERN (WHITE TERN) / SECHOSECH
Gygis alba candida   Laridae

L 31 cm, 12 in. Like the White-tailed Tropicbird, this graceful tern is often considered one of the world's most beautiful. It is nearly pure white, with a black eye-ring that gives it an endearing big-eyed look. The bill is deep blue at the base, black at the tip and unusually shaped for a tern. It is roughly dagger-shaped like a stretched-out triangle, with a slight upturn. Most people know this bird as the Fairy Tern, but the same name is also used for an unrelated tern found in southern Australia, so ornithologists coined the name White Tern for this one, and more recently the name Angel Tern. So far neither name has gained wide acceptance, and complicating the matter is the fact that "the" Fairy, White or Angel Tern may actually be 3 different species! So here we are using two alternative traditional English names. Palau's Fairy Terns belong to a subspecies (or species) that is found in the tropical Indian and Pacific oceans. There are other forms in the tropical Atlantic *G.a.alba* and in the northern Marquesas Islands *G.a.microrhyncha* in the eastern Pacific. They are among the most familiar and best-loved birds on tropical islands around the world.

The Fairy Tern is probably so named because of its graceful, fluttery flight and the fact that it tends to hover around people who get too close to the chick, often right in front of one's face. They do not attack and perhaps are attempting to lure away what they view as a predator. During these performances, they utter their harsh *grrich-grrich-grrich* calls which are as unattractive as the bird is lovely. The calls have twangy quality like the sound of a loose plucked string or rubber band. Although their low flight is rather butterfly-like, high over their nest trees Fairy Terns also engage in acrobatic swooping and diving, sometimes as small groups flying in formation, but they never form large flocks.

More than anything else, the Fairy Tern is know its remarkable nesting habits. Although it "nest trees, it builds no nest. Pairs shop together for s and walk back and forth over a prospective pla lay their brown-speckled egg. They often appe be pointing to particular spots with their bills whether they are really communicating this wa cannot say. The single egg is laid in a slight dep sion or a spot with just enough irregularities to vent it from rolling off the branch. Many pe assume the egg is fastened in some way, but it is The two parents take turns incubating and ch places without moving the egg. The chic equipped with extremely long claws that enable keep its place even in high winds (up to a point; of eggs and chicks are lost in storms). Young c are variably buffy with dark blotches, but ter become whiter with age. Eventually they bec fluffy balls of white down with big black eyes, even the most hardened scientist would have t them cute. The parents feed the chick tiny fis squid, which they pick from the ocean surface fa at sea, and bring back crosswise in the bill. Just they hold onto the first fish while catching anoth something of a mystery.

Thomas Dove

Juv

Michelle & Peter Wong

COMMON BLACK-HEADED GULL
Larus ridibundus Larid

L 41 cm, 16 in. This small species is the only gull recorded for certain in Palau, where it is a fairly regular winter visitor. They are most often seen around Malakal. The bill is heavier than that of terns and lacks the sharp tip. Adults are white with a pale gray back and characteristic black spot behind the eye, and show a white triangle in the outer primaries in flight. Legs and bill are red. In breeding plumage, rarely seen at Palau, the head is all dark. Immatures have a yellowish bill and legs, more black markings in the wings, and a black tip to the tail.

COMMON TERN
Sterna hirundo Larid

L 37 cm, 14.5 in. Like the previous species, this "common" bird is uncommon at Palau. It is only a rare passage migrant in spring and fall, and can turn up anywhere including freshwater ponds. The subspecies that migrates through Micronesia differs from Common Terns elsewhere in having the bill and feet black in all seasons. It is a graceful swallow-tailed tern with long tail streamers, whose outer webs are black. The breeding plumage, with a complete black cap, is not usually seen in Palau. The Common Tern is larger and darker than the Black-naped Tern, but the non-breeding plumage pattern closely resembles that of the shorter-billed Whiskered tern (next page). Common Terns always feed by plunge-diving, but Whiskered and Black-naped rarely do.

WHITE-WINGED TERN
Chlidonias leucopterus Larid

L 24 cm, 9.5 in. This marsh tern is an uncommon passage migrant at Palau. In non-breeding plumage, it closely resembles the Whiskered Tern (next page), but differs in that the rump is white, contrasting with the upper back, and the head pattern shows a black dot in the auriculars not connected around the nape except for a patch of gray streaks. The body is mostly black with the namesake contrasting wings in breeding plumage, but it has never been seen in Palau. Habits of White-winged and Whiskered terns are similar, and they may flock together. White-wings tend to be earlier migrants than Whiskered. The Malakal sewer ponds are a good place to spot them.

Deane P. Lewis

LITTLE TERN   W
Sterna albifrons   Laridae

L 23 cm, 9 in. This aptly-named Little Tern is the smallest in Palau. It is present in low numbers most winters and often favors paved areas such as runways and boat ramps. It is white below and pale gray above, with a contrasting pale rump and partial black cap. The cap is smudgy in nonbreeding and immature birds, but with a sharply defined white forehead in breeding adults. The bill and legs are black in most birds seen at Palau, but turn yellow, the bill with a black tip, as the nesting season approaches. Flying adults show a distinctive wing pattern with two black outer primaries. Little Terns hover and plunge-dive for food.

WHISKERED TERN   W
Chlidonias hybrida   Laridae

L 25.4 cm, 10 in. This species belong to a group called marsh terns because they breed in freshwater habitats in the northern hemisphere. Wintering birds are just as likely to be seen in shallow coastal waters. They differ from the Sterna terns in having shorter bills, shallowly forked tails, and feeding behavior that includes much more surface-picking than diving. They do not hover. This bird was unknown at Palau until HDP photographed one in 1993 on southern Babeldaob. Subsequently, the numbers each winter gradually increased, and now at least a few birds are present every year. They are mostly seen around freshwater habitats, such as Lake Ngardok or aquaculture ponds, but also feed in saltwater lagoons. Most birds seen are in nonbreeding plumage with dark bill and legs. They are gray above, white below, with a black crescent connecting the eyes around the nape, broader and less sharply defined than that of the Black-naped Tern. The plumage resembles that os the Common Tern, a larger bird with much more deeply forked tail and longer bill. Breeding Whiskered Terns are handsome birds with red bill and legs, entirely black cap, and slate-gray underparts that define the white "whiskers" below the cap. Sometimes, birds lingering in Palau into May exhibit full or partial breeding plumage as shown in the photo right.

233

BIRDS OF SURROUNDING SEAS AND OUTLYING ATOLLS

Palau's main islands are surrounded by the deep blue waters of the western Pacific Ocean. Many birds are found only in this habitat, and come to land or near land only for nesting. They are the true seabirds. The separation of these pelagic or marine birds from those of the lagoon is somewhat artificial because both inhabit saltwater habitats, but the distinction seems to make sense at Palau. Still, some "lagoon" birds (White-tailed Tropicbird, Bridled Tern, Fairy Tern) could just as easily have been placed here because they feed mostly at sea and are usually thought of as pelagic species. For this book, the distinction is whether the average observer would see the bird without venturing outside the reef. This section is for those birds that are rarely seen close to the main inhabited islands. This part of the Palau avifauna is very poorly known because few birders or ornithologists visit Palau's offshore waters and remote Southwest Islands. The few uninhabited islands, largely free of ground predators, are important seabird nurseries. They teem with terns, boobies, frigatebirds, and tropicbirds during an extended breeding season. Such islands are the key to survival for pelagic species, and rats, feral cats and dogs can completely destroy a nesting colony. Palauan fishermen know these birds well, although they do not know the identities of the rarer visitors. They often follow seabird flocks to locate schools of tuna and other predatory fish. The larger fish drive smaller ones to the surface, where they are attacked by birds from above and by large fish from below.

Palau's seabirds fall into three well-defined bird orders: 1) Procellariiformes, which include **shearwaters and petrels** Procellariidae and **storm petrels** Hydrobatidae at Palau, flying close to the water. One shearwater nests among the Rock Islands, but the others are visitors only. 2) Pelecaniformes. All four of their toes are connected by webs, and they have an expandable throat pouch. **Pelicans** Pelecanidae and **cormorants** Phalacrocoracidae are mainly inshore seabirds, discussed in the previous section, while the main marine groups at Palau include 2 species of **tropicbird** Phaethontidae, one included in the previous section, 3 **boobies** Sulidae, and 2 **frigatebirds** Fregatidae, most of which breed here. 3) Charadriiformes. This order at Palau includes rare **jaegers** Stercorariidae, aggressive pirates that steal food from other seabirds, **gulls** and 7 breeding species of **terns** Laridae, distinguished by their continuous flapping flight high off the water, and rare **phalaropes** Charadriidae, which are pelagic sandpipers.

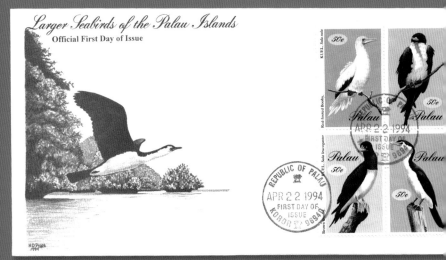

TROPICAL SHEARWATER/OCHAIEU
Puffinus bailloni   Procellariidae

L 31 cm, 12 in. Until recently this bird was known as Audubon's Shearwater, a bird with a pantropical dis
tribution, but DNA research has shown that the Pacific populations of "Audubon's" are actually a sepa
rate species. Tropical Shearwaters are neatly patterned black above and white below. At sea, they alter
nate rapid wingbeats and long glides, and at a distance seem to flash black and white as they show each
surface alternately. They also swim on the surface, sticking their heads under water to catch small fish
They also dive and even swim under water in pursuit of prey. They are not usually in flocks, but severa
may gather over a school of fish. Late in the day, however, they congregate in swirling groups that spira
upwards before birds begin to peal off and head directly to their roosting and nesting sites. Occasionally
a shearwater is downed on level ground, or flies into a boat, from which it cannot easily take off, and i
captured. One such bird is shown here.

Tropical Shearwaters at Palau breed throughout the year. They lay their white eggs in crevices on high
usually inaccessible, limestone cliffs in the Rock Islands. Tall islets off the western end of Urukthapel ar
a favored locality. They leave before sunset, and return when little light is left to see. A person in a boa
near one of the nest islands after dark may be treated to a delightful cacophony as returning birds utte
their eerie cries. The call is a two-part *shooo-kreeee*, like an inhale-exhale, with the first note raspy, the
second screechy. Hearing a chorus of such calls one can easily understand why superstitious early sai
ors thought they were the voices of demons. The ***ochaieu*** is a traditional god in Ngchesar State, alon
with the spotted eagle ray *Aetobatis narinari* which shares the same local name. The shearwater ap
pears on the state flag, and both animals are protected from hunting by both law and custom. Eve
today, Palauans believe harm will come to their clan if a member kills a shearwater or eagle ray.

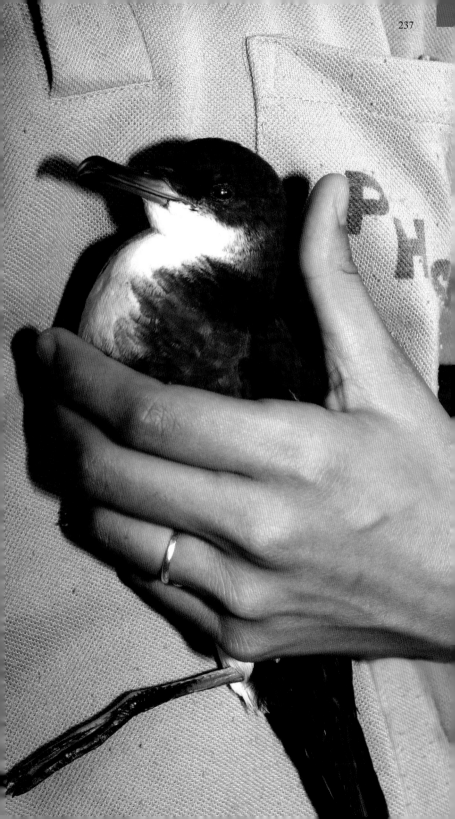

RED-TAILED TROPICBIRD
Phaethon rubricauda   Phaethontida

L 93 cm, 37 in. (tail streamers about half). Although this species is widespread in the Indian and Pacifi
Oceans, it was only recently confirmed to be breeding in Palau's Southwest Islands, and it may well b
a recent colonist as it is expanding its range elsewhere in Micronesia, turning up at several new localitie
in the past 2 decades. The first Palau records of the Red-tailed Tropicbirds were in the late 1970s on To
and Sonsorol in the Southwest Islands, and residents reported the birds were nesting on both islands b
the early 1990s. Red-tailed Tropicbirds feed far out to sea, and when not nesting may disperse widel
Recently one was seen off the coast of Babeldaob, so observers should watch for them around the mai
Palau islands also.

The Red-tailed Tropicbird looks all white at a distance, lacking the black dorsal markings of the smalle
White-tailed Tropicbird. It has a large bright red bill, black feet, and a black crescent in front of the ey
The body plumage is pearly or satiny, suffused with pale pink, which fades as the feathers age. But mos
strikingly, the two central tail feathers are white at the base and narrow into long slender spikes that hav
a black midrib and narrow red vanes (they look all-red at a distance). These two feathers are replace
constantly so that there is usually one long one and one still growing. Occasionally, a bird may lose bot
at once. The red feathers figure prominently in a spectacular courtship display flight over the nestin
area. Birds fly in circles, alternately flapping and gliding, until a small group, usually 2-5, begin flyin
backward in vertical circles, each bird vaulting over the others in turn, while holding the tail feathers dow
and swinging them back and forth. During all of this, the birds make a raucous squawking. Eventually, i
dividuals leave the group and land at prospective nest sites. Pairs return to the same spot year afte
year, and if one of them fails to return, the other will look for a new mate in the same colony.

These tropicbirds nest on the ground underneat[h] shading trees or bushes. The nest is only a sha[l]low depression in the sand from which debris h[as] been removed. Pairs lay a single brown-spott[ed] egg. Young hatchlings are covered in dark gr[ay] down, which whitens as the bird grows. Dow[n] chicks can be very defensive, making a har[d] raspy cry at the approach of a potential predat[or]. The female is very reluctant to leave the egg [or] chick, and when forced to fly off, will return w[ith] her mate to dive-bomb and try to scare off the p[o]tential predator. Body feathers appear first on t[he] back, heavily marked with black horizontal wa[vy] lines. The black barring remains through the fi[rst] year. The bill starts out black, and turns red as t[he] bird attains its adult feathering over a period [of] about two years. The chicks are fed regurgitat[ed] fish and squid, which are caught by plunge-divin[g]. A hunting bird hovers over a prospective cat[ch] then dives in after it. Tropicbirds do not sw[im] under water, so dives are not deep. Saw-tooth[ed] edges of the mandibles help hold the prey, whi[ch] is swallowed while the bird is floating on the s[ur]face.

BROWN BOOBY/ KUEL
Sula leucogaster   Sulida

L 76 cm, 30 in. The Brown Booby is a handsome bird, mostly dark chocolate brown with a white bel
and wing linings. The heavy, pointed bill varies from yellow to green, shading into dark blue (male)
yellow (female) at the base. Immature birds are patterned like adults, but the white is replaced by a pal
brown. The brown is the most likely booby to be seen off Palau's main islands, where a few can be see
feeding just outside the reef or resting on buoys. They roost at Kayangel, but do not nest there. The bi
gest concentration is in the Southwest Islands where a huge nesting colony is found on Helen Islan
and a smaller one on Fana.

Like other boobies, the Brown flies with alternating flaps and long glides, and may swing back and for
from wave to wave like a pendulum, revealing alternately the dark upper side and the white underpar
It fishes by plunge-diving. The birds circle high over a school of fish, then fold the wings back and ent
the water like a dart. They seem to favor flying fish, but also eat squid. Circling flocks of Brown Boobi
can be seen from a great distance, so they are popular with fishermen as an indicator of where tuna a
driving flying fish to the surface. They will often come and check out boats, flying overhead and som
times even landing on boats. As graceful as they are in the air, boobies are clumsy and rather goofy
looking on land, which caused early sailors to give them their unattractive name.

Brown Boobies are generally silent birds, but on their nesting grounds females give a harsh honking ca
and the male a quiet hissing whistle. Nesting occurs throughout the year, but the peak is in April-Ma
The nest is on the ground under trees, often surprisingly near the tide line, and is just a scrape in th
sand lined with dead leaves. They are often found nesting together with Red-footed Boobies and Bla
Noddies on the same beaches.

Each pair lays two yellow-brown eggs, and both usually hatch, but only one chick survives. Chicks are naked at hatching, but soon grow a coat of white down. They are fed by regurgitation, with the chick putting its bill into the parent's gular pouch. Chicks leave the nest well before they can fly, and walk around on beaches while still being fed by the adults. They often have to be herded back to the shade away from the water edge by the parents. The young birds are fearless of people and can easily be approached, but their parents are very protective. Chicks are vulnerable to both rats and dogs, not to mention local people who still today occasionally take them for food. Young birds are also sometimes brought to Koror from the Southwest Islands as pets, and when young can be trained to go out fishing during the day to return at night. Eventually, probably when ready to mate, the birds will disappear.

When short of food, people on remote atolls sometimes harass the nesting or roosting birds into throwing up their catch, which they will then eat themselves, just like the frigatebirds often do to the boobies in flight.

RED-FOOTED BOOBY/ KUEL
Sula sula   Sulidae

L 71 cm, 28 in. The Red-footed Booby is widely distributed in tropical oceans around the world. In Palau it is seen mostly near its nesting colonies on Fana and Helen Island. It occurs around the main islands much less than the Brown Booby, but sometimes roosts on Kayangel. Adult Red-footed Boobies come in a variety of colors, called morphs, which have nothing to do with age or sex (rather like blondes and brunettes among people). Only two of the morphs are usually seen at Palau. The white morph, which accounts for about 90% of Palau birds, is all white, including the tail, except for black primaries and secondaries. The dark feathers have a silvery look like they have been powdered. The other morph present is called white-tailed brown, in which the tail, belly and rump are white but the back and upper wing surface is dark brown, the head, neck, and breast light brown or buff (below). Both morphs have blue bill with a pink base, thinner than the bills of Brown Boobies and, of course, bright red feet. Juvenile and immature birds, identified by their black bills, are all dusty brown at first, which gradually lightens over a period of 2 years. Juvenile Red-foots lack the sharp 2-tone pattern of young Brown Boobies. Adults of the white morph could be confused with the rare Masked Booby, which is also mostly white, but the Masked has a black tail and the black of the secondaries is broad where it meets the body, whereas the Red-foot's black tapers to a point inwardly. At a distance against the dark sea, a Red-foot looks like a flying white triangle, while a Masked looks like a flying white cross.

Red-foots feed at sea out of sight of land. Their prey capture methods are similar to those of the Brown Booby, with spectacular plunge dives from great heights. They mainly eat flying fish and squid, and their large eyes aid them after dark when squid rise to the ocean surface, but they are not primarily nocturnal feeders.

Red-footed Boobies nest throughout the year, and some adults are always present in the breeding colonies, but there is a distinct peak in the spring months and a lull in the fall. Unlike other boobies, Red-foots nest and roost exclusively in trees, where they build a substantial nest of sticks, grass, and leaves. Residents of Sonsorol say that roosting birds sometimes kill trees with their weight and guano. Courtship involves a display called sky-pointing, in which the bill points straight up, the tail is raised, and the wings are raised at the elbow so that the primaries also point skyward. A loud squawk accompanies this display. Much of the ritual involves building the nest. The male brings the materials, and the female builds. When the male flies in with a stick, he utters a series of low croaks that speed up, then slow down. Both birds sky-point frequently and also bow to each other. Pairs may remain together for many years. The single egg is white, and is incubated for a little over 6 weeks. The hatchling is naked and pink, then gray, but white down begins to grow immediately and the chick soon becomes a fluffy white ball. Chicks eat regurgitated food from the adult bill. The chicks remain in the nest until they fledge at the age of just over 3 months.

immature ♂

GREAT FRIGATEBIRD
KEDAM
Fregata minor   Fregati

L 93 cm, 37 in. Frigatebirds take their names from a
of sailing ship formerly used by pirates. That is beca
they often steal food from other birds, especially
bies. Frigatebirds pursue and harass their victims
they throw up their catch, then the frigatebird catch
in midair before it hits the water. Such behavior is c
kleptoparasitism, and though it is characteristic of
atebirds, they actually catch most of their food for th
selves. They catch flying fish in midair, or small fis
squid swimming near the surface. The 5 species of
atebird are widespread in the world's tropical oce
but are relatively scarce in Micronesia. Only 2 spe
have been recorded in Palau, with the Greater far m
common than the Lesser Frigatebird. They are
rarely seen around the main islands, but roost in
Southwest Islands and on Kayangel. They nest on
Fana and possibly Merir in the Southwest Islands,
many, if not most, of the frigatebirds seen in Palau
have come from nesting colonies in the outer islan
Yap or elsewhere.

Frigatebirds are conspicuous and unmistakable.
often fly very high up in the sky and their long na
wings appear to have a kink at the wrist. Their tail
very deeply forked, providing superb maneuvera
but are often folded into a point. Their aerial skill
unequalled in the bird world, and they have the gre
ratio of wing area to weight of any birds. They can
on thermals or in light winds for hours with little pe
tible wing motion. When they do flap, as when
calm or they are in pursuit, their wing beats are
and powerful, and their tails enable them to m
sudden acrobatic twists and turns when necessar
though their feet are narrowly webbed, frigate
almost never sit on the water because unlike m
other marine birds, their feathers are not waterpro

immature

♀

♂

A swimming frigatebird risks becoming wat
logged and unable to take off again. Their feet a
proportionately very small, and virtually usele
on land, so frigatebirds almost never land on
ground either.

Their plumages are confusing. They go throug
molt sequence that can produce some very od
looking variations. Adult male Great Frigatebi
are entirely black. Adult females have a wh
chest and a gray throat. Juveniles of both se
have the head and chest rusty red, the ch
darker, and a white belly separated from the ch
by a black "belt". The belt gradually disappears
the bird gets older. Immatures have a white he
and chest, with some rusty color retained in
throat. Bill color varies from pink to gray.

Their stick nests are placed high in trees, althou
sometimes low shrubbery is used where there
no human presence. The male steals nesting
terial from booby nests to build his own, and wh
the nest is ready, the male sits on it and condu
a vigorous mating display that involves infla
his bright red gular pouch, spreading and shak
his wings, and uttering a low-pitched whinny.
inflated gular pouch looks like a big red ball
hanging from the bird's throat, and is inflated a
deflated at will within minutes. Females will ci
overhead, and several females may come do
to the nest at the same time and fight over v
gets to mate with the most popular males. La
ing on the nests is a major undertaking for
large birds with their enormous wings, and th
have to be careful not to get caught in branche
fall to the ground where it would be hard for th
to fly off between the trees.

Nesting takes place from January until Aug
and they lay one white egg. The chick hatc
naked and helpless, and develops a coat of w
down in 1-2 weeks. Both parents care for
chick, which grows very slowly, requiring
months to fledge. As a result, individual frig
birds do not nest every year, and when not n
ing, they disperse widely from their breeding si
Young Frigatebirds on their first flights someti
get tangled in tree branches, resulting in a bro
wing and certain death. If landing on the w
surface close to shore, tiger sharks han
around waiting for nesting turtles have b
known to attack them.

Eric VanderWerf

Michelle & Peter Wong

H.Douglas Pratt

LESSER FRIGATEBIRD
Fregata ariel   Fregatid

L 76 cm, 30 in. This bird is less common at Palau a
smaller than the Great Frigatebird, and whether it ne
here regularly is questionable. Adult males have t
white patches on the sides under the wings. Fem
have the entire head black including the throat. Exc
for a single sighting off Peleliu, they are found only
Helen Island, and their numbers fluctuate year to ye
Only one nest has ever been seen on Helen (Ow
1977a), so a lot of the birds reported are from colon
elsewhere in the tropical Pacific. The breeding biol
of this bird is similar to that of the Great Frigatebird, a
the two are often found in the same nesting colonies

RED-NECKED PHALAROPE   W
Phalaropus lobatus   Charadriid

L 20 cm, 8 in. When MTE recently photographed t
bird swimming in the Rock Island lagoon near Ulc
Island, ornithologists did not know that the Red-neck
Phalarope was in Palau, although its wintering grour
include the seas north of New Guinea. This photogra
will document the first record for Palau (details to
published elsewhere), but interestingly when s
showed the photo to her Palauan husband and his fi
ing buddies, they were familiar with the bird, and
marked that it swims around in circles like a drunk, w
out in the open ocean, a perfect description of a pela
phalarope. They see phalaropes 20-50 miles outs
the reef, where birders almost never go, so Palau m
well be part of the bird's regular wintering area. Pha
ropes eat insects and plankton by spinning in circles
the water surface, their feet stirring up organisms. Th
plumage is like that of a duck, providing a layer
trapped air on which they float. The name comes fr
the breeding plumage when the front and sides of
bird's neck are rusty red. Phalaropes are close relativ
of sandpipers, despite their love of the open sea.

LONG-TAILED JAEGER
Stercorarius longicaudus   Larid

L 55 cm, 22 in. It has a rather ternlike flight, and
rasses smaller seabirds. Thought to be a scarce
grant through the tropics, its habits are poorly knowr
has been seen several times near Palau.

MASKED BOOBY
Sula dactylatra   Sulid

L 81 cm, 32 in. Larger than Palau's other 2 breec
boobies and with a dark tail, it is seen mostly far ou
sea. The closest breeding area is in the Mariana Is.

Eric VanderWerf

•OTY TERN   I
rna fuscata   Laridae

cm, 17 in. The Sooty Tern resembles the Bridled
, but is entirely black above with the black cap con-
ted to the dark back, and a white wedge on the fore-
d. Juvenile birds are all black except for white under
tail and pale wing linings, and may be mistaken for
dies. This is one of the most pelagic of terns, spend-
most of its life flying over tropical and subtropical
s. It virtually never lands on water because its plum-
has little waterproofing, but it may briefly perch on
am, and only comes to land to nest in densely
ked colonies. Amazingly, young Sooty terns are
ight to spend as much as two years in the air after
ging, before coming to some remote island to nest,
ch at Palau is Helen Island. The size of this abun-
t colony varies during the year, with some birds
ays present and in some stage of nesting. The nest
shallow depression in the sand, where a single
ted egg is laid. Downy chicks are buff with dark
ckles and can run almost immediately. Frigatebirds
known to take many chicks, and the adults have
defense against them or people, rats, dogs and
. Chicks can fly in about ten weeks. These birds are
ly seen around Palau's main islands. They feed by
ing items off the water surface, or catch small fish in
air when they leap out of the water. At sea they are
ally seen in flocks.

H Douglas Pratt

TSUDAIRA'S STORM PETREL   W
anodroma matsudairae   Hydrobatidae

cm, 10 in. Palau's only storm petrel nests on Kita
ima in Japan's Volcano Is. and spends the non-
ding season mostly in the Indian Ocean. It migrates
ugh western Micronesia, and is seen occasionally in
uan waters. It is a small dark seabird with a long
ed tail, and flies close to the water with flapping and
ng. It picks up food from the surface while holding
rings well above the horizontal.

H.Douglas Pratt

DGE-TAILED SHEARWATER   V
inus pacificus   Procellariidae

cm, 17 in. Rare in Palau, this shearwater is the
t abundant shearwater in the tropical Pacific. It has
and dark color morphs, but all those seen in Palau
ar have been dark birds. They are probably visitors
further south, where dark morphs predominate.
eral other all-dark shearwaters could potentially
ir near Palau, including the Flesh-footed, which is
er with pale feet. Other dark shearwaters tend to
their wings straight out, rather than bowed forward
the Wedge-tailed, and some have pale wing linings.

Eric VanderWerf

BATS

Most oceanic islands, such as those that make up Palau, have what scientists call disharmonic faunas. That means that many of the groups of animals that one would routinely expect to find on a continent are not present, as if in an orchestra, one had strings but no woodwinds. One of the most conspicuous gaps on islands is the near total absence of land mammals. Land mammals simply are not well equipped to cross large distances across salt water. The one exception is bats, which have similar dispersal powers to birds. Bats are the only mammals with true flight (such things as sugar gliders, flying squirrels, and flying lemurs only glide). Palau has two living species, representing the two main worldwide subdivisions of the Order Chiroptera: the larger Megachiroptera, known as fruit bats or flying foxes, found in the Old World tropics; and the smaller Microchiroptera, which are nocturnal, insectivorous, and found worldwide. Both groups have similar-looking wings, but the details are different and DNA studies have revealed that the two groups are not closely related, and that flight probably evolved independently in each. Bat wings are the structural equivalent of human hands, with a web of skin (called a patagium) stretching between the fingers. The thumb (digit 1) is not connected to the patagium, and is used mainly when the animals perch. Digits 2 and 3 lie close together, so the main part of a bat's wing is supported by digits 3 and 5. In small bats, only the thumb has a claw, but fruit bats have a small claw on the second digit as well. A patagium also connects the hind legs and tail. The hind feet have their toes directed backward, and the claws can thus be used to hang upside down from a perch. Insectivorous bats can actually walk a bit on a flat surface, but those at Palau are not very good at it. They are almost exclusively creatures of the air, and are amazingly precise in their aerial maneuvers. The larger fruit bats fly very differently, with deep wing beats that resemble those of a night heron.

There is one other native mammal, the dugong *Dugong dugon* locally called **mesekiu**. A few other mammals were introduced by man, and none are beneficial. They include 3 species of rats, one mouse, one shrew, and the long-tailed macaque. Palau also has far too many feral cats and dogs, and some wild pigs.

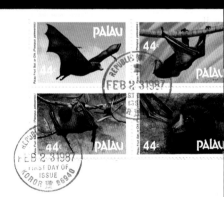

OFFICIAL   FIRST   DAY   COVER

POLYNESIAN SHEATH-TAILED BAT/ CHESISUALIK

Emballonura semicaudata   Emballonuridae

Sheath-tailed bats are so named because their tails protrude from the surrounding skin a shor distance, as if out of a sheath. This species is widespread in the tropical Pacific, from Palau to Samoa. I is the only representative of the small insect-eating and echolocating bats, known as *Microchiroptera*, in Palau. At one time, the Palau population was regarded as an endemic subspecies, but modern refer ences do not distinguish it from populations in the Marianas and Polynesia. In many places (as in the Marianas), these little bats have declined drastically, and now are nearly extirpated. The Palau popula tion, thankfully, seems to be thriving, perhaps because they have many safe places to roost away from human disturbance, especially in the limestone caves of Airai and the Rock Islands.

Sheath-tailed bats are cave dwellers, and the Rock Islands of Palau provide abundant caves and rock overhangs. During the day, the bats roost in large clusters of dozens to hundreds of individuals, clinging to the sides and roof of the cave, often in the darkest reaches. Despite the old saying "blind as a bat" bats are not blind, but their eyes are small compared to their ears, and they depend on hearing for mos navigation and feeding. They find their way in the gloom of caves by using echolocation, similar to sona or radar. They make high-pitched sounds that bounce off the cave walls and back to their large and highl sensitive ears. How this works when dozens of bats are flying at once is a mystery, but they seldom co lide with each other. Most of the sounds made by small bats cannot be heard by humans, but we ca hear some of the lower-pitched ones. They sound like a light twittering, but are actually quite loud when measured by sound-detecting equipment. Roosting sheath-tailed bats are easily disturbed, and will f around in the caves if humans intrude.

Sheath-tailed bats also use echolocation to hunt insects on the wing. They leave their caves at dusk to begin their nightly foraging. This is the time when most people see them, although it is also the time when they are most easily mistaken for swiftlets. These bats eat nearly any kind of flying insect, including mosquitoes, and thus perform a very useful service. In former times, they were a common sight flying around street lights in Koror to feed on the insects attracted there, but recently they are seen much less often. Perhaps the roost caves closer to town are too often visited by people and the bats have abandoned them in favor of more remote locations. Although they roost communally, sheath-tailed bats usually hunt alone, so they are not often seen flying together in large numbers.

Female sheath-tailed bats are larger than males. They give birth upside down, and the young bats cling to their mother for some time, which may explain the need for larger size. These bats often share caves with swiftlets.

PALAU FRUIT BAT/ OLIK

Pteropus pelewensis   Pteropodida

The Palau Fruit Bat, also called Palau Flying Fox, is variously classified either as an endemic species a subspecies of *P.Mariannus* (which has representatives on all the high islands of Micronesia). It is a typ cal fruit bat in every way, lacking the ability to echolocate and having large eyes for nocturnal flight. It ha an endearing fox-like face, can be tamed if captured young, and might have become a popular pet exce for its unpleasant odor. We can enjoy them at a distance, however, because they are a conspicuous pa of Palau's environment. Visitors from temperate regions where fruit bats are not found are often shocke to see a bat so large, and one that can be easily seen in daylight. They are found throughout the main i lands of Palau.

Palau Fruit Bats feed on a wide variety of fruits, and are important in the forest ecosystem as seed di persers. They also take nectar from flowers, some of their favorites being the indigenous tree called **dc** ironwood *Intsia bijuga*, the **rebotel** Wax apple *Eugenia javanica* and the **mesekerrak** Java plum *Euger cumini*. The bats seem to know when the trees are about to flower and gather in them in large congrega tions for several days. Bats engage in a lot of squabbling over good flower clusters. Individuals defei flowers against interlopers by clapping their wings, which makes a sound that can be heard from 15 distance. But most of the diet is fruit rather than nectar, and all kinds are eaten. The only time fruit ba come into towns and villages in Palau is when certain trees are in fruit. They are fond of non-native fru such as mango, as well as local figs *ficus spp.*, **remiang** cycad *Cycas circinalis* and **ongor** pandan *Panadanus spp*. The bats' fine teeth enable them to extract the sweet pulp at the base of the tough brous pandanus keys.

Palau Fruit Bats are plagued by ectoparasitic *Cyclopodia albertisii*, which can be seen in the p on the next page, top left. Otherwise, fruit bats few natural threats, but humans can be ser predators to them. Palauans traditionally ate bats, catching them at night with triangular *sigero* fastened to long poles, wielded from a form built in the trees. Although fruit bats have been a popular food item with Palauans in re years, they are considered a great delicacy and tural icon among the Chamorros of the Marian lands, and in the 1970s and 1980s, over one hun thousand fruit bats were exported from Pala Guam (where residents there had eaten their fruit bats to near extinction). Fortunately for the p pects of Palau Fruit Bats, that trade has now cea A few Koror restaurants still serve fruit bat, mos Japanese tourists. The bat is cooked whole served in a clear broth, not very appetizing to we tastes.

A second species, the Large Palau Fruit Bat *P pus pilosus*, is known from two specimens colle in Palau before 1874. Recent searches have fail find it, and it is presumed extinct. The reason fo disappearance are unknown.

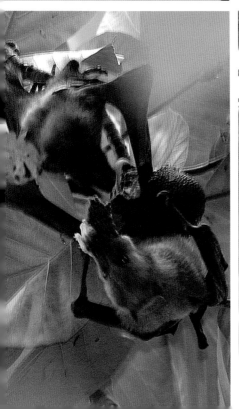

Fruit bats often gather in favored trees to sun themselves in the morning. Palauans refer to this a *oremuul ra olik*. Such a gathering in a *Casuarina* tree on Angaur is shown on the next page, these wer all females , most of them pregnant or with young clinging to them. When they get too hot, they open an flap their wings, which are heavily endowed with blood vessels. Likewise, when they get too cool, the use their wings like a blanket to wrap their whole body. They also use the wings as a waterproof raincoa While they can be seen any time of day, fruit bats become most active in late afternoon when large roos ing congregations begin to break up. They forage individually, although many may gather at a good foo source, and spend the night in those trees. On southern Babeldaob at dusk the sky is often filled wi hundreds of bats headed in different directions. In the Rock Islands, they can often be seen fighting wi starlings over ripe breadfruits during the day.

For some reason, male and female fruit bats do not seem to get along well, and they segregate at roost They come together only for mating, and even that seems more like a rape than a romantic encounte Females give birth to one, or rarely two, young that cling to her until they are able to forage on their own They suckle from teats located in the "armpits" and learn the flavors of the "right" fruits by licking the mother's mouth. Female young seem to stay with the mother a lot longer than males, and can be almo the same size as their mother while still clinging onto her as long as she allows it. The oldest known Fru Bat kept in captivity on Palau since his birth was a 28 year old male.

About the photographs

Thomas Dove
Thomas Dove is an Army Physician currently stationed in Iraq. During a 20 year assignment in Hawaii
visited Micronesia on many occasions providing care to heart patients throughout the region. His bird ph
tographs were featured in the recent Hawaii Audubon publication "Birds of Hawaii" and other publicatio

I enjoy taking pictures of all birds, but I spend most of my time now traveling to take pictures of waders
use a Nikon D2X camera with a 1.4 teleconverter and a Nikon 600mm F4 lens. There is nothing mag
about Nikon, in fact I yearn for the Image stabilization offered by Canon on its long lenses, but I alrea
had several Nikon lenses. A sturdy tripod is a must for me with shorebirds, with this much magnificati
even a little vibration will result in a blurry image. I use a Glitzo 1325 Carbon Fiber tripod (light and sturc
with a Wimberly Gimbal style pivoting head, which allows me to track moving birds with this 12-pou
setup. At slower shutter speeds vibration from the mirror can be transmitted to the lens. You can put an a
on the lens to dampen those vibrations. Despite the imposing size of this camera setup shorebirds need
be approached quite closely to get dramatic images. There is no substitute for knowing your subject, a
how close they will allow you to approach. When approaching a bird I always take a few images after ea
step in case the bird takes off. Most of the best photographers are not above crawling in the mud, whi
has 2 benefits. You can approach more closely, and the eye-to-eye perspective of a low camera angle c
be quite striking. The additional benefit is a soft background of ocean or sky. Patience is a virtue reward
in bird photography, and a long lens is a must. A 300mm would be the absolute minimum unless you a
shooting a tame bird. Always be prepared for the unexpected. On my last trip to Palau, Mandy and I we
anchored off a beach for lunch, when a Megapode walked out on the beach 40 feet in front of us and calr
started digging a huge hole in the sand, totally ignoring us. I was able to get several shots of this funny b
with a tripod from the boat while he slowly disappeared into his hole. Whatever he was doing, perfecti
his digging technique or chasing a very stubborn crab, the very a-typical behavior of this bird made my d

Mandy T. Etpison
I'm a Canon fan myself, and for this book I used a 30D and a EOS-1DMark II (I prefer the lighter a
simpler 30D). My favorite bird lenses are my EF100-400 USM and the 500mm USM, the latter I use wit
monopod and 1.4 teleconverter (thanks, Tom!). Since I'm usually hiking through the Rock Islands, tripc
don't work well for me. My favorite subjects are the endemic forest birds, as well as boobies, they alwa
make me laugh with their goofy behavior, like the fearless chick on the next page whose mother w
circling anxiously above. The custom function on my 30D camera I use most is the flash sync fixed 1/2
speed in Av mode, so I can change the depth of field and keep the fast shutter speed. This works v
inside the jungle, when the lighting is bad and I'm trying to get a moving bird. The AI Servo AF mode w
high-speed continuous shooting works for flying birds in a clear sky, but I still find that a real challenge fr
a moving boat. Manual focus is a must inside the forest with moving birds, where vines and leaves
close around or blocking part of the subject. Using autofocus will usually get you a sharp leaf but a fu
bird. I love those rare moments when a bird finally sits still when I'm ready and actually have the right le
on. There is nothing as frustrating as a normally shy bird landing right in front of your face when you sta
there with a 600mm lens on your camera... Locating a nest is always a treat. I enjoy watching a bi
behavior around its nest, from the feisty little Flycatcher, attacking anything that comes too close to its n
to the shy Fruit Dove, abandoning its nest and chick at the slightest disturbance. Observing nests
taught me a lot about different bird behavior, and how to best approach them for photos in general.

I know you probably want to hear all sorts of technical details about the photos in this book, but you'd
horrified to learn how little I actually know. I'll just say that an artistic eye, determination, a lot of patien
and learning from my many mistakes and fuzzy photos ultimately got me the 670+ photos you see in
book. I still haven't figured out most of the features on the Mark II camera body, and probably never
Lacking the natural grace and stealth all islanders seem to have for maneuvering through a jungle, I a
rely heavily on the co-operation of the subjects, since they can hear me coming from a mile away...

BIRD PHOTO BASICS

- Focus on the eyes, and shoot at bird's level or lower
(even if this means climbing a tree or lying flat on your belly)
- Use a lens in the 300- 600mm range for waders and flying birds
- A 100-400 zoom lens is more flexible inside a jungle and on a hike
- Be patient, wait for feeding or unusual behavior, and try different angles
- Try for a contrasting plain background,
or use a large aperture to blur a busy one.
- Do not clear around nests for a better picture, this will attract predators,
and move away from the nest if the parent birds do not return after 15 minutes.

Thomas Dove

Shallum Etpison

STATUS AND CONSERVATION OF BIRDS IN PALAU
by Eric VanderWerf

The first detailed descriptions of the avifauna of Palau were by Kramer (1908-1910) in German, an
Momiyama (1922) in Japanese. During and after World War II, much new information came to lig
(Marshall 1949, Baker 1951) and Rollin Baker's monograph remains an important basic reference toda
Robert P. Owen, Chief Conservationist for the Trust Territory of the Pacific Islands, was stationed in Kor
during the 1970s, and made the first continuous multi-year bird observations in Palau. He was joined
1977 by John Engbring, then with the U.S. Peace Corps, who greatly increased knowledge of the loc
birds (Engbring 1883, 1988; Engbring and Pratt 1985; Pratt et al.1980). In 1991, under the auspices of th
U.S. Fish and Wildlife Service, he conducted the first quantitative assessment of the overall status of bir
in Palau (Engbring 1992). Angela Kepler (1993) made additional surveys in the Southwest Islands.
2004-2005, the Palau Conservation Society organized systematic surveys and inventories to assess th
conservation status of Palau's birds, with assistance of BirdLife International, the U.S. Fish and Wildli
Service, and the U.S. Peace Corps. This effort facilitated identification of Important Bird Areas (IBAs)
Palau and measurement of the distribution and abundance of most of Palau's bird species (VanderWerf
al. 2006, VanderWerf 2007).

The goal of the IBA program (www.birdlife.org/action/science/sites/index.html) is to identify geograph
areas that support globally or regionally important bird populations, using internationally agreed upon a
scientifically defensible criteria. IBAs may be chosen because they hold birds that are threatened, enda
gered, or restricted to particular regions or biomes, or because they support large concentrations of migr
tory birds during some part of the year. Birds are good indicators of overall biodiversity and ecosyste
health, and identification of IBAs can help to prioritize areas for protection and conservation action. Mo
extensive analysis of the survey data is underway and will provide estimates of population density an
population size for each species by island. Anecdotal observations can provide some important clue
about the local abundance of birds and about areas that harbor important populations of particular specie
but quantitative surveys, such as those conducted in 1991 and 2005, are necessary to provide informati
on the overall status and trends of bird populations throughout Palau.

Much of Palau has retained a substantial portion of the native avifauna, but several areas are particula
important and warrant careful protection. The Rock Islands contain some of the most intact habitats
Palau and support several rare or restricted-range species, and are already protected as a natu
preserve. The iconic Ngerukuid Islands are the most protected region in Palau and have the highest abu
dance of several bird species, indicating this high level of protection has helped sustain healthy bird pop
lations. Peleliu is a very important island because it has high avian diversity in general, supports importa
populations of several species that have vey limited ranges, and several species are more abundant
Peleliu than elsewhere. The extensive tidal mudflats around the northern end of Peleliu attract lar
numbers of migratory shorebirds. Babeldaob supports the largest populations of many bird speci
because of its large size, and the more remote parts of Babeldaob contain the largest remaining blocks
native forest habitat, such as along the Rael Kedam or central ridge that runs north to south in the inter
of the island, along the western ridge in western Ngardmau and Ngaremlengui, and in the Ngerutec
region of southern Ngaremlengui. The Lake Ngardok Conservation Area is the largest freshwater wetla
in Palau, supports the rare Pacific Black Duck and largest population of Common Moorhens, and is
important stopover site for a variety of migratory water birds (VanderWerf et al. 2006). Ngeriungs Island
Kayangel supports an important concentration of the Micronesian Megapode. The Southwest Islands
Palau, particularly Fana and Helen, hold large breeding colonies of many seabirds that are among
most important in the region.

Bird Monitoring. In order to assess whether any of Palau's birds are threatened or declining, and wheth
conservation efforts are effective, it will be necessary to continue monitoring the status of bird populatio
over time and in different areas, using the same techniques that have been employed before, and a
more specialized monitoring methods. Based on surveys in 1991 and 2005, several bird species appea
have declined in abundance in the Rock Islands. The cause(s) of these declines are mysterious becau
the Rock Islands are among the least disturbed and most protected areas in Palau. There is evidence t
several seabirds declined in Palau from 1991-2005, including Black and Brown Noddies and Fairy Ter

ese species are still common and face no immediate survival risk, but the cause of these apparent clines is unknown and warrants further investigation.

ome species and groups of birds, particularly coastal, wetland, and nocturnal species, have not been dequately surveyed in Palau. The surveys conducted in 1991 and 2005 were designed primarily to onitor the endemic and resident avifauna of Palau. Most of these species live in forests and savannahs, survey routes were deliberately located in these habitats. Many areas of coastal marine and freshwater abitat were not surveyed, and the status of their birds is not well known. Monitoring of coastal and wetland rds will require different techniques that focus on these habitats. No bird surveys have been conducted night in Palau, so the status of the nocturnal Palau Owl and Gray Nightjar are poorly known. They can reliably found in certain areas, but their overall distribution and abundance remain undocumented, so cannot say whether they may be declining or under threat.

ndangered Species. Most species of birds in Palau appear to be stable, but some species are rare and hers appear to be declining, so there is cause for some concern. Several Palau birds are considered eatened or endangered by various agencies and organizations. The International Union for the Conser- tion of Nature (IUCN) considers the Micronesian Megapode to be endangered, and the Nicobar Pigeon, alau Ground Dove, Micronesian Imperial Pigeon, and the Giant White-eye to be near threatened ww.iucnredlist.org). Three Palau species, the Palau Ground Dove, Palau Owl, and Palau Fantail, were rmerly listed as endangered under the U.S. Endangered Species Act (USFWS 1970), but they were moved from the list in 1985 (USFWS 1985). Three other species, the Nicobar Pigeon, Blue-faced Parrot- ch, and White-breasted Woodswallow, were once considered for listing under the U.S. Endangered ecies Act, but they are no longer candidates. The Republic of Palau has its own list of species of national ncern, and 8 bird species have been proposed for inclusion: Pacific Black Duck, Micronesian (Palau) egapode, Nicobar Pigeon, Palau Ground Dove, Palau Owl, Palau Fantail, Blue-faced Parrotfinch, and hite-breasted (Palau) Woodswallow. Palau's birds face several threats, the most serious of which are bitat loss and alteration, invasive species, and hunting. The severity of these threats varies among ecies and in different parts of Palau.

abitat Loss and Alteration. Loss of habitat is perhaps the most important threat to birds worldwide. For- nately, Palau has experienced only a moderate amount of habitat loss because development has, until cently, occurred on a relatively small scale and has been concentrated in a few areas. Most of the habitat ss has occurred in the extensive urbanized areas of Koror, Malakal, and southwestern Babeldaob, where ost of Palau's people live. There was serious habitat destruction in some areas of Palau during World ar II, particularly on Peleliu, but the damage was temporary and native habitats have mostly recovered.

wever, development in Palau has accelerated recently, and loss and degradation of habitat now threat- s birds over a larger area than ever before. Construction and improvement of roads in many aeas of lau, particularly the Compact Road that now encircles Babeldaob, has resulted in large-scale loss of tive forests and savannahs. Erosion of exposed soil in road cuts is likely to cause additional habitat loss, d the resulting downstream siltation threatens birds in wetland and coastal habitats. Surveys in 2005 owed that most of the species that have declined since 1991 live primarily in forests, indicating that forestation may already be affecting some birds. These early stages of decline should serve as a rning that better habitat protection and greater sensitivity to environmental impacts during development now needed to help maintain Palau's valuable natural ecosystems.

e increased development on Palau has resulted in conversion of native forest and savannah to second- forest, gardens, plantations, and open grassy areas. This habitat alteration has been detrimental to the jority of native bird species, but there are a few birds that have benefited. The Buff-banded Rail, Micro- sian Myzomela, and Black-headed Munia favor open habitats, and appear to have increased in abun- nce from 1991 to 2005. The myzomelas are adaptable and forage on flowers of a variety of plant ecies, including ornamental garden varieties. The munia, a non-native bird, may have benefited from d construction in particular because it feeds primarily on seeds of alien grasses in open areas, and this bitat has become abundant along most of the length of the Compact Road.

asive Species. Non-native, or alien, species that are introduced to an area by humans and then rease in number and range, displacing native species, are said to be invasive. Such species pose a eat to many birds worldwide, and can be especially insidious on islands, where native species often ve no defenses against new predators, competitors, and diseases. For example, the brown tree snake *iga irregularis*, a voracious predator native to northern Australia, New Guinea, and adjacent islands, was cidentally introduced to Guam in the late 1940s or early 1950s and has since caused the loss of 10 of 13 native forest bird species on the island (Savidge 1987, Wiles et al. 2003). Every effort should be made to ensure that this snake never reaches Palau because it would endanger not only birds, but ba[...] geckos, skinks and native snakes as well. Rats of several species have become serious predators of bir[...] and bird nests on many Pacific islands, especially those used by nesting seabirds. Measures should [...] taken to prevent the spread of rats to currently rat-free islands within Palau. Invasive alien species such [...] feral pigs, cats and monkeys are present in some of Palau's forests and may be responsible for reduc[...] bird abundance and diversity.

Hunting. Although it is illegal, hunting of Micronesian Pigeons and Nicobar Pigeons, both regarded as de[...] cacies, still goes on in Palau. In recent surveys on Babeldaob, Micronesian Pigeons were common in me[...] remote areas farther from human populations, but uncommon or absent near towns and roads, suggest[...] their abundance is still affected by hunting. Abundance of the Nicobar Pigeon actually increased from 19[...] to 2005, but the total population of this species in Palau remains too small to withstand sustained huntir[...] The restriction on use of shotguns in Palau likely has decreased hunting pressure, but increases in hum[...] population and greater access to forested areas through road construction may have the opposite effe[...] Micronesian Pigeons and Nicobar Pigeons have become rare elsewhere in their ranges, due in part [...] hunting. Palau is now one of their strongholds, and they should be protected here.

Acknowledgements. The bird surveys and conservation status assessment conducted in 2005 were org[...] nized by the Palau Conservation Society and were funded by BirdLife International, the U.S. Fish a[...] Wildlife Service, and the Seaworld-Busch Gardens Conservation Fund (through the U.S. Peace Corps[...]

.s annotated list is intended as both a "literature cited" and a list mportant standard references for anyone wishing to gain addi─al information about Palau's birds and bats. The general refer─ces were consulted during the writing of this text, but only spe─c bird records or similar facts are cited (author/ date).

ker, R. H. 1951. The avifauna of Micronesia, its origin, evolu─, and distribution. University of Kansas Publications of the seum of Natural History. 3:1-359

ptista, L. F., P. W. Trail, and H. M. Horblit. 1997. Family umbidae (pigeons and doves). Pp.60-243 in del Hoyo, J., El─:, A., and Sargatal, J. eds. (1997). Handbook of Birds of the rld. Vol.4. Sandgrouse to Cuckoos. Lynx Edicions, Barcelona.

dLife International. 2000. Threatened birds of the world. ─x Edicions and BirdLife International, Barcelona & Cambridge, .

kland, C., and H. Manner, EDS. 1989. Resource survey of ─erukewid Islands Wildlife Preserve, Republic of Palau. Report he Government of Palau, the South Pacific Environmental Pro─m, World Wildlife Fund, and the International Union for the ─nservation of Nature and Natural Resources. University of ─am, Mangilao.

─utigam, A., and T. Elmqvist. 1990. Conserving Pacific ─nd flying foxes. Oryx 24:81-89

─ner, P. L., and H. D. Pratt. 1979. Notes on the natural his─ and status of Micronesian bats. 'Elepaio 40:1-4.

─yns, W. F. J. M. 1964. Birds seen during west to east trans─ific crossing along equatorial counter-current around latitude in the autumn of 1960. Sea Swallow 17:57-66.

─antler, P. and G. Driessens. 1995. Swifts. A Guide to the ─fts and Treeswifts of the World. Yale University Press, New ─ven, CT.

kinson, E. C., Ed. 2003. The Howard and Moore complete ─cklist of the birds of the world. 3rd edition, revised and en─ed. Princeton University Press, Princeton, NJ.

─jbring, J. 1983. Avifauna of the Southwest Islands of Palau. l Research Bulletin 267:1-22

─jbring, J. 1988. Field guide to the birds of Palau. Conserva─Office, Koror, Palau.

─jbring, J. 1992. A 1991 Survey of the Forest Birds of the Re─ic of Palau. US Fish & Wildlife Service, Honolulu, Hawaii.

─jbring, J. and R. P. Owen. 1981. New bird records for Mi─esia. Micronesica 17:186-192

─bring, J. and H. D. Pratt. 1985. Endangered birds in Mi─esia: their history, status, and future prospects. Bird Conser─n 2:71-105.

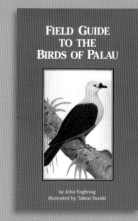

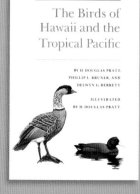

PELEW-EILANDERS.
FROM DE MENSCH - AMSTERDAM. 1803.

Etpison, M. T. 1997. *Palau: portrait of paradise.* Neco Marir Corp., Koror, Palau.

Etpison, M. T. 2004. *Palau-Natural & Cultural History.* Tk Corp. Koror, Palau.

Flannery, T. F. 1995. *Mammals of the south-west Pacific & M luccan Islands.* Cornell University Press, Ithaca, N.Y.

Gauger, V. H. 1999. Black Noddy (*Anous minutus*). *In* The Bird of North America, No. 412 (A. Poole and F. Gill, Eds.)

Gibbs, D., E. Barnes, and J. Cox. 2001. *Pigeons and doves: guide to the pigeons and doves of the world.* Yale Univers Press, New Haven and London.

Gill, F., and M. Wright. 2006. *Birds of the World: Recommen ed English names.* Princeton University Press, Princeton a Oxford.

Harrison, P. H. 1983. *Seabirds: an identification guide.* Houg ton Mifflin Co., Boston, MA.

Jenkins, J. M. 1983. The native forest birds of Guam. Ornith logical Monographs No.31.

Jones, D., R. W. R. J. Dekker, and C. S. Roselaar. 199 *The megapodes.* Oxford University Press, Oxford, U.K.

Kepler, A. K. 1993. Terrestrial biota of the Southwest Palau lands, western Pacific. technical report, Bureau of Resources a Development, Republic of Palau.

Keate, G. 1803. *An Account of the Pelew Islands.* Fifth Editi London. With added Supplement by J.P.Hockin, compiled fr the journals of the vessels Panther and Endeavour.

Kramer, A. *Ergebnisse der Sudsee-expedition 1908- 1910. Mikronesien. Palau, vol 1-5.* Hamburg, 1917- 1929.

Lee, W.-S.,T.-H. Koo, and J.-Y. Park. 2000. *A field guide the birds of Korea.* LG Evergreen Foundation, Seoul, Sou Korea.

Madge, S., and H. Burn. 1988. *Waterfowl: An identificat guide to the ducks, geese, and swans of the world.* Bosto Houghton Mifflin Co.

Marshall, J. T., Jr. 1949. The endemic avifauna of Saipa Tinian, Guam, and Palau. Condor 51: 200-221.

Mayr, E. 1945. *Birds of the southwest Pacific.* Macmillan C New York.

Message, S. and D. Taylor. 2005. *Shorebirds of North Ameri Europe, and Asia.* Princeton University Press, Princeton & Oxf

275

Metz, V. G., and E. A. Schreiber. 2002. Great Frigatebird (*Fregata minor*). *In* The Birds of North America, No.681 (A.Poole and F. Gill, Eds.) The Birds of North America, Inc. Philadelphia, PA.

Momiyama, T. 1922. *Birds of Micronesia*. Ornithological Society of Japan.

Owen, R.P. 1977a. New bird records for Micronesia and major island groups in Micronesia. Micronesica 13:57-63.

Owen, R. P. 1977b. A checklist of the birds of Micronesia. Micronesica 13: 65-81

Perez, G. S. A. 1968. Notes on Palau fruit bats. Journal of Mammalogy 49: 758.

Perez, G. S. A., and H. T. Kami. 1967. Report on the observations of Micronesian Pigeons and some marine and wildlife resources of Palau. Division of Fish and Wildlife, Department of Agriculture, Guam.

Pregill, G. K.& D. W. Steadman. 2000. Fossil vertebrates from Palau, Micronesia: a resource assessment. Micronesica 33: 137-52.

Pyle, P., and J. Engbring. 1985. Checklist of the birds of Micronesia. 'Elepaio 46: 57-68.

Pyle, P., and J. Engbring. 1987. New bird records and migrant observations from Micronesia, 1977-1984. 'Elepaio 47: 11-16.

Pratt, H. D., J. Engbring, P. L. Bruner, and D. G. Berrett. 1980. Notes on the taxonomy, natural history, and status of the resident birds of Palau. Condor 82: 117-131.

Pratt, H. D., P. L. Bruner, and D. G. Berrett. 1987. *A field guide to The Birds of Hawaii and the Tropical Pacific*. Princeton University Press, Princeton, N.J.

Savage, J. A. 1987. Extinction of an island forest avifauna by an introduced snake. Ecology 68: 660-668.

Schreiber, E. A., and R. W. Schreiber. 1993. Red-tailed Tropicbird (Phaethon rubricauda). *In* The Birds of North America, No.43 (A.Poole and F.Gill, Eds.). Philadelphia: The Academy of Natural Sciences; Washington, D.C.: The American Ornithologists' Union.

Schreiber, E. A., R. W. Schreiber, and G. A. Schenk. 1996. Red-footed Booby (*Sula sula*). *In* The Birds of North America, No.241 (A.Poole and F.Gill, Eds.). Academy of Natural Sciences, Philadelphia, PA., and American Ornithologists' Union, Washington, DC.

1783 observations by the crew of the British ship Antelope:

As to birds, they had plenty of undomesticated common cocks and hens that ran about the woods; and what will appear singular, considering their little variety of food, they had never made any use of them... yet when they went into the woods, they frequently eat their eggs; but they did not admire them for being newly laid; the luxury to them was, when they could swallow an imperfect chicken in the bargain!

Pigeons they had also in the woods. At the time of breeding they took the young from the nest, keeping them on a perch tied by one leg, and feeding them on yams: this bird was accounted a great dainty, and none but those of a certain dignity permitted to eat thereof. The people of Pelew were wonderfully active and expert in climbing up trees in quest of these nests.

The islands had also several small birds, whose notes were very melodious, particularly one which used to sing every morning and evening, and had a pipe sweet as a flagelet: our people often thought they were under the very tree whence the notes of this little bird came, yet none of them were ever certain they had seen it.

Keate, G. 1803
An Account of the Pelew Islands

276

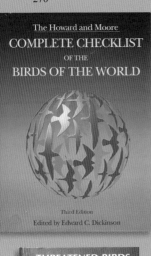

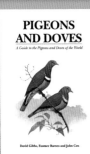

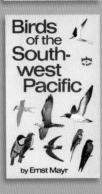

Schreiber, E. A., C. J. Feare, B. A. Harrington, B. G. Murra
Jr., W. B. Robertson, Jr., M. J. Robertson, and G.
Woolfenden. 2002. Sooty Tern (*Sterna fuscata*). *In* The Birds
North America, No.665 (A. Poole and F. Gill, Eds.). The Birds
north America, Inc, Philadelphia, PA.

Shimba, T. 2008. *Photographic guide to the birds of Japan a.
North-east Asia*. Yale University Press, New Haven, CT.

Taylor, P. B. 1998. *Rails: A Guide to the Rails, Crakes, Ga
nules, and Coots of the World*. Yale University Press, New Hav

Tetens, A. 1958. *Among the Savages of the South Seas. Me.
oirs of Micronesia, 1862-1868*. Stanford and London.

U.S. Fish and Wildlife Service. 1970. Conservation of enda
gered species and other fish or wildlife. Federal Register 35 (10
8491-8498.86

U.S. Fish and Wildlife Service. 1985. Determination
remove three Palau birds from the list of endangered and thre
ened wildlife. Federal Register 50 (177): 37192-37194.

VanderWerf, E. A.,G. J. Wiles, A. P. Marshall, and
Knecht. 2006. Observations of migrants and other birds
Palau, April-May 2005, including the first Micronesian record c
Richard's Pipit. Micronesica 39:11-29.

VanderWerf, E. A. 2007. 2005 Bird surveys in the Republic
Palau. Report submitted to the Palau Conservation Society a
the U.S. Fish and Wildlife Service. Pacific Rim Conservation, H
nolulu, Hawaii.

Wiles, G. J. 2005. A checklist of the birds and mammals of
cronesia. Micronesica 38:141-189.

Wiles, G. J., and P. J. Conry. 1990. Terrestrial vertebrates
the Ngerukewid Islands Wildlife Preserve, Palau Islands. Mic
nesica 23: 41-66.

Wiles, G. J., and P. J. Conry. 2001. Characteristics of n
mounds of Micronesian Megapodes in Palau. Journal of Field
nithology 72: 267-275.

Wiles, G. J., D. J. Worthington, R. E. Beck, Jr., H. D. Pr.
C. F. Aguon, and R. L. Pyle. 2000. Noteworthy bird records
Micronesia, with a summary of raptor sightings in the Mariana
lands, 1988-1999. Micronesica 32: 257-284.

Wiles, G. J., J. Bart, R. E. Beck, Jr., and C. F. Aguon. 20
Impacts of the brown tree snake: patterns of decline and spec
persistence in Guam's avifauna. Conservation Biology 17: 135
1360.

Wiles, G. J., N. C. Johnson, J. B. De Cruz, G. Dutson, V
Camacho, A. K. Kepler, D. S. Vice, K. L. Garrett, C. C. K.
sler, and H. D. Pratt. 2004. New and noteworthy bird reco
from Micronesia, 1986- 2003. Micronesica 37: 69-96.

CHECKLIST OF THE BIRDS AND LAND MAMMALS OF PALAU

Note: Status code as in main text; E= endangered, C= conservation concern, **E**= endemic species, **e**= endemic subspecies, **I**= indigenous resident species, **A**= alien introduced, **M**= spring & fall migrant , **W**= winter migrant, **V**= irregular visitor. with addition of **X** for extinct species and **R** for species based on one, few, or old records and unlikely (but not impossible) to be seen again in Palau. Gray entries have not been published in a scientific journal. Question marks indicate uncertain data or localities. Headings: **K**= Kayangel; **KB**= Koror & Babeldaob; **R**= Rock Islands; **P**= Peleliu; **A**= Angaur; **SW**= Southwest Islands; **O**= Surrounding oceans.

CLASS AVES: BIRDS

				K	KB	R	P	A	SW
	MEGAPODES	MEGAPODIIDAE							
E e	Palau Megapode	*Megapodius laperouse senex*	*bekai*	X	X	X	X		
	CHICKEN-LIKE BIRDS	PHASIANIDAE							
A	Red Junglefowl	*Gallus gallus*	*malkureomel*	X	X	X	X	X	X
	WATERFOWL	ANATIDAE							
V	Eurasian Wigeon	*Anas penelope*	*debar*		X				
E I	Pacific Black Duck	*Anas superciliosa*	*debar*		?			?	
W	Northern Pintail	*Anas acuta*	*debar*		X		X	X	
W	Garganey	*Anas querquedula*	*debar*		X		X	X	
W	Eurasian Teal	*Anas crecca*	*debar*		X		X	X	
W	Tufted Duck	*Aythya fuligula*	*debar*		X		X	X	
	PETRELS, SHEARWATERS	PROCELLARIIDAE							
R	Providence Petrel	*Pterodroma solandri*							
V?	Bulwer's Petrel	*Bulweria bulwerii*							X
V	Streaked Shearwater	*Calonectris leucomelas*							
V	Wedge-tailed Shearwater	*Puffinus pacificus*							
I	Tropical Shearwater	*Puffinus bailloni*	*ochaieu*		X	X			
	STORM-PETRELS	HYDROBATIDAE							
M	Matsudaira's Storm-Petrel	*Oceanodroma matsudairae*							
	TROPICBIRDS	PHAETHONTIDAE							
I	White-tailed Tropicbird	*Phaethon lepturus*	*dudek*	X	X	X	X	X	X
I	Red-tailed Tropicbird	*Phaethon rubricauda*	*dudek*		X				X
	BOOBIES	SULIDAE							
V	Masked Booby	*Sula dactylatra*	*kuel*						X
I	Brown Booby	*Sula leucogaster*	*kuel*	X					X
I	Red-footed Booby	*Sula sula*	*kuel*	X					X
	PELICANS	PELECANIDAE							
R	Australian Pelican	*Pelecanus consicillatus*		X	X	X	X	X	X
	CORMORANTS	PHALACROCORACIDAE							
I	Little Pied Cormorant	*Phalacrocorax sulcirostris*	*deroech*						
R	Little Black Cormorant	*Phalacrocorax sulcirostris*							
	FRIGATEBIRDS	FREGATIDAE							
I	Great Frigatebird	*Fregata minor*	*kedam*	X	X				X
I	Lesser Frigatebird	*Fregata ariel*	*kedam*				X		X
	HERONS, EGRETS, ETC	ARDEIDAE							
I	Yellow Bittern	*Ixobrychus sinensis*	*cheloteachel*		X	X	X	X	
R	Von Schrenk's Bittern	*Ixobrychus eurhythmus*			?				
V	Gray Heron	*Ardea cinerea*			X		X		
W	Great Egret	*Ardea alba*	*sechou*		X		X		
W	Yellow-billed Egret	*Egretta intermedia*	*sechou*		X	X	X	X	
W	Little Egret	*Egretta garzetta*	*sechou*	X	X		X	X	X

			K	KB	R	P	A	SW	O
Pacific Reef Heron	*Egretta sacra*	**sechou**	X	X	X	X	X	X	X
Cattle Egret	*Bubulcus ibis*	**keremlal sechou**	X	X	X	X	X	X	X
Striated Heron	*Butorides striatus*			X					
Black-crowned Night-Heron	*Nycticorax nycticorax*			X					
Rufous Night-Heron	*Nycticorax caledonicus*	**melabaob**		X	X	X	X		
Japanese Night-Heron	*Gorsachius goisagi*			X					
Malayan Night-Heron	*Gorsachius melanolophus*			?					
HAWKS	ACCIPITRIDAE								
Osprey	*Pandion haliaetus*					X	X		
Black Kite	*Milvus migrans*			X			X		
Brahminy Kite	*Haliastur indus*				X				
Chinese Sparrowhawk	*Accipiter soloensis*			X	X			X	
Gray-faced Buzzard	*Butastur indicus*			X					
FALCONS	FALCONIDAE								
Peregrine Falcon	*Falco peregrinus*			X					
RAILS, MOORHENS, COOTS	RALLIDAE								
Red-legged Crake	*Rallina fasciata*			?					
Slaty-legged Crake	*Rallina eurizonoides*	**ulerratel**		X	X	X	X		
Buff-banded Rail	*Gallirallus philippensis*	**terriid**	X	X	X	X	X		
Rufous-tailed Bush-hen	*Amaurornis moluccanus*								X
White-browed Crake	*Poliolimnas cinereus*	**sngorech**		X		X	X		
Purple Swamphen	*Porphyrio p. pelewensis*	**uek**		X		X	X		
Common Moorhen	*Gallinula chloropus*	**debar**		X		X	X		
PLOVERS	CHARADRIIDAE								
Gray Plover	*Pluvialis squatarola*			X		X		X	
Pacific Golden Plover	*Pluvialis fulva*	**derariik**	X	X	X	X	X	X	X
Lesser Sand Plover	*Charadrius mongolus*			X		X	X	X	
Greater Sand Plover	*Charadrius leschenaultii*			X		X	X	X	
Snowy Plover	*Charadrius alexandrinus*			?					
Common Ringed Plover	*Charadrius hiaticula*			X					
Little Ringed Plover	*Charadrius dubius*			X		X		X	
Oriental Plover	*Charadrius veredus*					X		X	
Red-Kneed Dotterel	*Erythrogonys cinctus*			X					
STILTS	RECURVIROSTRIDAE								
Black-winged Stilt	*Himantopus himantopus*		X	X		X			
SANDPIPERS, SNIPE	SCOLOPACIDAE								
Common Greenshank	*Tringa nebularia*			X		X	X	X	
Marsh Sandpiper	*Tringa stagnatilis*			X		X	X		
Common Redshank	*Tringa totanus*			X		X			
Wood Sandpiper	*Tringa glareola*			X		X	X	X	
Green Sandpiper	*Tringa ochropus*			X					
Wandering Tattler	*Heteroscelus incanus*			X					
Gray-tailed Tattler	*Heteroscelus brevipes*		X	X	X	X	X	X	
Common Sandpiper	*Actitis hypoleucos*	**bengobaingukl**	X	X	X	X	X	X	
Terek Sandpiper	*Xenus cinereus*			X					
Little Curlew	*Numenius minutes*			X				X	
Whimbrel	*Numenius phaeopus*	**okak**	X	X	X	X	X	X	
Eastern Curlew	*Numenius madagascariensis*			X	X	X			
Black-tailed Godwit	*Limosa limosa*			X		X		X	
Bar-tailed Godwit	*Limosa lapponica*			X		X		X	
Ruddy turnstone	*Arenaria interpres*		X	X	X	X	X	X	
Great Knot	*Calidris tenuirostris*			X		X			
Red Knot	*Calidris canutus*			X					
Sanderling	*Calidris alba*			X					
Red-necked Stint	*Calidris ruficollis*		X	X	X	X	X	X	
Long-toed Stint	*Calidris subminuta*			X			X		

				K	KB	R	P	A	SW
M	Pectoral Sandpiper	*Calidris melanotos*			X				
M	Sharp-tailed Sandpiper	*Calidris acuminata*			X		X	X	
V	Dunlin	*Calidris alpina*			X				
V	Curlew Sandpiper	*Calidris ferruginea*			X		X		
R	Broad-billed Sandpiper	*Limicola falcinellus*						X	
M	Ruff	*Philomachus pugnax*			X		X		
M	Swinhoe's Snipe	*Gallinago megala*			X			X	?
W	Red-Necked Phalarope	*Phalaropus lobatus*				X			
	PRATINCOLES	**GLAREOLIDAE**							
M	Oriental Pratincole	*Glareola maldivarum*			X				
	GULLS, TERNS, JAEGERS	**LARIDAE**							
V	Long-tailed Jaeger	*Stercorarius longicaudus*			X				
W	Common Black-headed Gull	*Larus ridibundus*			X				
I	Swift Tern	*Sterna bergii*	**roall**	X	X	X	X	X	X
I	Black-naped Tern	*Sterna sumatrana*	**kerkirs**	X	X	X	X	X	X
V	Little Tern	*Sterna albifrons*			X				
R	Spectacled Tern	*Sterna lunata*							
I	Bridled Tern	*Sterna anaethetus*	**bedebedechakl**	?	X				
I	Sooty Tern	*Sterna fuscata*		?					X
M	White-winged Tern	*Chlidonias leucopterus*			X		X		
W	Whiskered Tern	*Chlidonias hybrida*			X				
I	Brown Noddy	*Anous stolidus*	**mechadelbedaoch**	X	X	X	X	X	X
I	Black Noddy	*Anous minutus*	**bedaoch**	X	X	X	X	X	X
I	Angel (White) Tern	*Gygis alba*	**sechosech**	X	X	X	X	X	X
	DOVES, PIGEONS	**COLUMBIDAE**							
C e	Nicobar Pigeon	*Caloenas nicobarica pelewensis*	**laib**		X	X	X		
C E	Palau Ground Dove	*Gallicolumba canifrons*	**doldol, omekrengukl**		X	X	X	X	
E	Palau Fruit Dove	*Ptilinopus pelewensis*	**biib**		X	X	X	X	
e	Micronesian Imperial Pigeon	*Ducula oceanica monacha*	**belochel**		X	X	X		
	PARROTS, COCKATOOS	**PSITTACIDAE**							
A	Sulphur-crested Cockatoo	*Cacatua galerita*	**iakkotsiang**		X	X			
A	Eclectus Parrot	*Eclectus roratus*	**iakkotsiang**		X	X			
	CUCKOOS	**CUCULIDAE**							
R	Chestnut-winged Cuckoo	*Clamator coromandus*			X				
R	Northern Hawk-Cuckoo	*Hierococcyx hyperythrus*			X				
V	Common Cuckoo	*Cuculus canorus*			?				
W	Oriental Cuckoo	*Cuculus saturatus*	**charmudrenges**	X	X	X	X	X	X
R	Brush Cuckoo	*Cacomantis variolosus*			X				
R	Pacific Long-tailed Cuckoo	*Eudynamys taitensis*			?				
	OWLS	**STRIGIDAE**							
E	Palau Owl	*Pyrroglaux podargina*	**chesuch**		X	X	X	X	
V?	Brown Hawk-Owl	*Ninox scutulata*							X
	NIGHTJARS	**CAPRIMULGIDAE**							
e	Gray Nightjar	*Caprimulgus indicus phalaena* **chebacheb**			X	X	X		
	SWIFTS	**APODIDAE**							
E	Palau Swiftlet	*Aerodramus pelewensis*	**chesisekiaid**		X	X	X		
	KINGFISHERS	**ALCEDINIDAE**							
e	Rusty-capped Kingfisher	*Todiramphus cinnamominus pelewensis* **cherosech**		X	X	X			
e	Collared Kingfisher	*Todiramphus chloris teraokai* **tengadidik**		X	X	X	X	X	X
	BEE-EATERS	**MEROPIDAE**							
R	Rainbow Bee-eater	*Merops ornatus*							X

			K	KB	R	P	A	SW	O
ROLLERS	**CORACIIDAE**								
Dollarbird	*Eurystomus orientalis*				X		X		
HONEYEATERS	**MELIPHAGIDAE**								
Micronesian Myzomela	*Myzomela rubratra kobayashii*	**chesisebangiau**	X	X	X	X	X		
WOODSWALLOWS	**ARTAMIDAE**								
Palau Woodswallow	*Artamus leucorynchus pelewensis*	**mengaluliu**			X	X			
CUCKOO-SHRIKES	**CAMPEPHAGIDAE**								
Palau Cicadabird	*Coracina tenuirostris monachum*	**kiuidukall**			X	X	X		
WHISTLERS	**PACHYCEPHALIDAE**								
Morningbird	*Colluricincla tenebrosa*	**tutau**			X	X	X		
SHRIKES	**LANIIDAE**								
Brown Shrike	*Lanius cristatus*						X		X
FANTAILS	**RHIPIDURIDAE**								
Palau Fantail	*Rhipidura lepida*	**melimdelebteb, chesisirech**			X	X	X		
MONARCHS	**MONARCHIDAE**								
Palau Flycatcher	*Myiagra erythrops*	**charmelachull**			X	X	X		
SWALLOWS	**HIRUNDINIDAE**								
Barn Swallow	*Hirundo rustica*	**tsubame**	X	X	X	X	X	X	
Asian House Martin	*Delichon dasypus*			X			X		
OLD WORLD WARBLERS	**SYLVIIDAE**								
Palau Bush Warbler	*Cettia annae*	**wuul, chesisebarsech**			X	X	X		
Lanceolated Warbler	*Locustella lanceolata*								X
Oriental Reed Warbler	*Acrocephalus orientalis*				X				
OLD WORLD FLYCATCHERS	**MUSCICAPIDAE**								
Siberian Rubythroat	*Luscinia calliope*				X				
Narcissus Flycatcher	*Ficedula narcissina*				?				
Gray-streaked Flycatcher	*Muscicapa griseisticta*				X	X	X		X
Blue Rock Thrush	*Monticola solitarius*				X				
THRUSHES	**TURDIDAE**								
Scaly Thrush	*Zoothera dauma*				X				
Eyebrowed Thrush	*Turdus obscurus*				X				
WHITE-EYES	**ZOSTEROPIDAE**								
Citrine White-eye	*Zosterops s. semperi*	**charmbedel**			X	X			
Dusky White-eye	*Zosterops finschii*	**chetitalial**			X	X	X		
Giant White-eye	*Megazosterops palauensis*	**charmbedel**			X	X	X		
STARLINGS, MYNAS	**STURNIDAE**								
Micronesian Starling	*Aplonis opaca orii*	**kiuid**			X	X	X	X	
Chestnut-cheeked Starling	*Sturnus philippensis*				?				
WAGTAILS, PIPITS	**MOTACILLIDAE**								
Yellow Wagtail	*Motacilla flava*		X	X	X	X	X	X	
Gray Wagtail	*Motacilla cinerea*				X				
White Wagtail	*Motacilla alba*				X				
Red-throated Pipit	*Anthus cervinus*				X		X		
Richard's Pipit	*Anthus richardi*				X				
BUNTINGS	**EMBERIZIDAE**								
Black-headed Bunting	*Emberiza melanocephala*				X				

				K	KB	R	P	A	SW
	OLD WORLD SPARROWS	PASSERIDAE							
A	Eurasian Tree Sparrow	*Passer montanus*			X		X		
	ESTRILDID FINCHES	ESTRILDIDAE							
e	Blue-faced Parrotfinch	*Erythrura trichoa pelewensis*			X	X	X		
A	Black-headed Munia	*Lonchura atricapilla*	**kanaria**		X				

CLASS MAMMALIA; MAMMALS

				K	KB	R	P	A	SW
	SHREWS	SORICIDAE							
A	House Shrew	*Suncus murinus*							X
	FRUIT BATS	PTEROPODIDAE							
E	Palau Fruit Bat	*Pteropus pelewensis*	**olik**		X	X		X	X
X	Large Palau Fruit Bat	*Pteropus pilosus*			?				
	SHEATH-TAILED BATS	EMBALLONURIDAE							
E	Polynesian Sheath-tailed Bat	Emballonura semicaudata	**chesisualik**	X	X	X	X		
	OLD WORLD MONKEYS	CERCOPITHECIDAE							
A	Long-tailed Macaque	Macaca fascicularis	**monkii, sukrii**		X			X	
	PIGS	SUIDAE							
A	Feral pig	Sus scrofa	**babiiureomel**		X				
	OLD WORLD RODENTS	MURIDAE							
A	Pacific Rat	Rattus exulans	**beab**	X	X	X	X	X	X
A	Asian House Rat	Rattus tanezumi	**beab**	X	X	X	X	X	X
A	Norway Rat	Rattus norvegicus	**beab**		X				
A	House Mouse	Mus musculus	**beab el ulemachell**	X	X	X		X	X

INDEX

Main species accounts are **boldfaced**. Numbers in *italics* indicate illustrations only.

THE AUTHORS

H. Douglas Pratt, Ph.D.

Dr. H. Douglas Pratt is the senior author and illustrator of *A Field Guide to the Birds of Hawaii and the Tropical Pacific*. He was born in Charlotte, NC, USA and attended Davidson College and Louisiana State University, where he earned his Ph.D. in 1979. During the ensuing 25 years as a Research Associate of the LSU Museum of Natural Science, he worked independently as an ornithological consultant, bird illustrator, and leader of birding tours. In 2005, he returned to his home state to become Research Curator of Birds at the North Carolina State Museum of Natural Sciences, where he continues his Pacific bird research. Dr. Pratt is a pioneer in the recording of Palau birds. He also designed Palau postage stamps depicting native birds for many years following postal independence. He has visited Palau a dozen times, most recently with a research group in April 2007. He is currently revising the Hawaii/ Tropical Pacific field guide for Princeton University Press and working on several scientific papers that will involve Palau birds. Dr. Pratt is a Fellow of the American Ornithologists' Union and an Associate of the Cornell Lab of Ornithology.

Daphne Gemmill

Mandy Thijssen Etpison

Born and raised in the Netherlands, Mandy lived in the Philippines before visiting Palau in 1984. She returned to work as the first PADI Open Water Scuba Instructor at the Palau Pacific Resort a few months later, and has worked with the Neco Group of Companies ever since. Her artwork and photography on Palau's wildlife and culture can be seen around Palau in hotels, brochures, art posters, murals, Palau stamps, nature ID cards, and books. She self-published several books on Palau, and her last book set, *Palau-Natural & Cultural History*, was published in 2004. In 1998, Mandy and her husband Shallum founded and built the Etpison Museum & Gallery on Koror, a private museum which showcases Micronesian history and culture to the public, and gives free admission to all Palauans and local schools. Mandy is Managing Director of the museum, has been a President appointed board member and Vice-chairperson of the Palau Visitors Authority from 2001-2007, and is Honorary Consul of France for the Republic of Palau.

Shallum Etpison

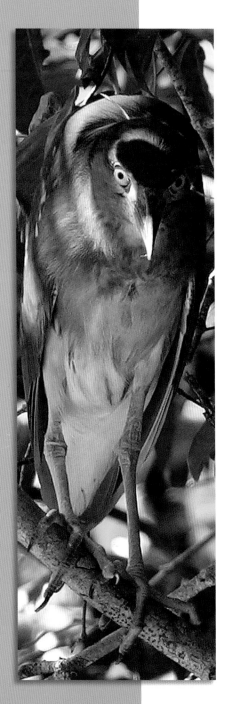

*T*he Rufous Night Heron is locally called Melebaob. When spelled Delebaob this describes someone who does things lazily, awkwardly, and inefficiently, comparing them to this large but clumsy bird.